Kate Atkinson's
*Behind the Scenes
at the Museum*

CONTINUUM CONTEMPORARIES

Also available in this series

Forthcoming in this series:

· **KATE ATKINSON'S**

*Behind the
Scenes at the
Museum*

A READER'S GUIDE

EMMA PARKER

CONTINUUM | NEW YORK | LONDON

2002

The Continuum International Publishing Group Inc
370 Lexington Avenue, New York, NY 10017

The Continuum International Publishing Group Ltd
The Tower Building, 11 York Road, London SE1 7NX

www.continuumbooks.com

Printed in the United States of America

Library of Congress Cataloging-in-Publication Data

Parker, Emma.
    Kate Atkinson's Behind the scenes at the museum : a reader's guide /
Emma Parker.
        p. cm.—(Continuum contemporaries)
    Includes bibliographical references.
    ISBN 0-8264-5238-8 (alk. paper)
    1. Atkinson, Kate. Behind the scenes at the museum. 2. Yorkshire
(England)—In literature.   I. Title. II. Series.
    PR6051.T56 B4437 2002
    823'.914—dc21
                                            2002000994
ISBN 0-8264-5238-8

Contents

For Charles Vander Zwaag, with love

Acknowledgements

Thanks are due to Kate Atkinson and Bryony Lavery for their generous help and cooperation. I am also indebted to Juliet Matthews at The Marsh Agency and Columbia University in New York, where I completed this book as a Visiting Scholar. Thanks to Graham and Rose Parker for archival research on the *Daily Mail*, Clare Anderson for providing me with a space to live and work, Ruth Corran for good vibes and, most of all, Charles Vander Zwaag for his invaluable insight and support.

1

The Novelist

When Kate Atkinson's publisher requested details about her life for marketing purposes, she provided a characteristically playful response that reveals her distaste for literary biography:

I've actually done quite a lot of interesting things but unfortunately I've forgotten most of them. I have a chronically bad memory. You'll just have to make stuff up. . . . If it was left to me, I'd write "Kate Atkinson was born in Yorkshire in 1951. She has lived half her life in Scotland. She has two daughters and has forgotten just about everything else."

Despite her elusiveness, this statement reveals some of the things that most preoccupy Atkinson: memory, imagination, home, motherhood, and (through a resistance to biography that implicitly attempts to shift attention away from the writer) her work.

Atkinson was indeed born in Yorkshire in 1951, the only child of parents who ran a medical and surgical supplies shop. Her father descended from coal miners, her mother from a family of railway workers. Fiercely aspirational, they sent their daughter to a private primary (or preparatory) school, where she became Head Girl. At

Queen Anne Grammar School for Girls in York, she shone academically whilst developing an interest in drama. In 1967 she auditioned (unsuccessfully) for the National Youth Theatre and in 1970 went to read English at Dundee University. She married a fellow student in 1973 and gave birth to her first daughter, Eve, the following year. After graduating with a Master's degree in 1974, she stayed at Dundee to do research on American postmodern fiction but, to her profound dismay, was finally refused a doctorate. Leaving Dundee without a PhD, she undertook a variety of jobs including legal secretary, welfare benefits administrator, home help, creative writing tutor on a community education program, and eventually returned to Dundee University to teach English. She had another child, Helen, with a Scottish teacher who she married in 1982. Atkinson has lived variously in York, Dundee, and Whitby. Twice divorced, she now lives in Edinburgh with her two daughters where she is busy "making stuff up."

Atkinson began writing short stories in 1981, shortly after the birth of her second daughter and the devastation of failing her doctorate. This setback functioned as a catalyst for her creative writing as it sparked the need to prove herself, not to the world, but to herself. Although being refused a PhD was a painful disappointment, it is now an experience she views philosophically, believing that she would not otherwise have become a writer. Thus out of failure came good fortune. Atkinson never showed her earliest fiction, a combination of autobiography and therapy, to anyone until she entered the *Woman's Own* short story competition in 1988. "In China," her first genuinely non-autobiographical story, won first prize. She still regards this event, which marked her formal decision to become a writer, as one of the best of her life. For the next few years Atkinson scraped a living writing commercial magazine fiction inbetween an array of other jobs, choosing short stories as her form precisely because their brevity enabled her to combine writing with the demands of being a single mother. When she turned forty, she decided to devote herself to writing full-time and, as a mark of her seriousness, procured an accountant. More success followed when "Snow Feathers" was announced runner up in the Bridport Arts competition in 1990 and "Karmic Mothers = Fact or Fiction?" won the prestigious Ian St. James Award in 1993. She found a publisher for *Behind the Scenes* soon after this, and transformed a series of short stories that had sat in a drawer for three years into a prize-winning international bestseller in just three months. It had been her ambition to finish it before she died.

A tragicomic novel that spans five generations of women, *Behind the Scenes at the Museum* (1995) is a humorous and moving chronicle of English family life. The main chapters follow the development of the irrepressible protagonist and narrator, Ruby Lennox, from her unglamorous conception in 1951, through disappointment, misery, and tragedy to the point at which she finds self-fulfillment forty years later. The novel focuses on Ruby's bitter relationship with Bunty, her irascible and undemonstrative mother, and her struggle to come to terms with repressed memories of trauma. As Ruby undergoes the process of self-discovery, a subtle and emotionally powerful exploration of loss, loneliness, grief, and regret is seamlessly combined with amusing accounts of farcical family conflict. The footnotes that follow each chapter swoop back to the 1890s via two World Wars, placing Ruby's experience in a broader historical perspective. Through these flashbacks Ruby tells the stories of her female antecedents — her great, great-grandmother, Sophia; her great-grandmother, Alice; her grandmother, Nell, and her own mother, Bunty — whose lives are defined by marital strife and domestic drudgery. The juxtaposition of past and present provides valuable insights into Ruby's own experience and makes visible historical continuities as well as significant points of change in the lives of women from different eras. *Behind the Scenes at the*

Museum won the Whitbread First Novel and Book of the Year Award in 1995, the Boeker Prize in South Africa, and was awarded the Livre Book of the Year in France. It was included in the American Library Association's Notable Books List in 1997 and was selected by Waterstone's Booksellers as one of the greatest ninety-nine novels of the previous ninety-nine years at the close of the century.

Atkinson's second novel, which she regards as her best, is close to the first in spirit but more ambitious in scope. Whereas *Behind the Scenes* harks back to Roman times, *Human Croquet* (1997) returns to the beginning of the world in its opening pages and closes with a vision of its end. Set against this vast canvas, most of the novel is set in Arden, home of the central character, Isobel Fairfax. Together with her brother, Charles, Isobel strives to make sense of the mysterious disappearance of her mother, Eliza, who vanished during a family picnic in the forest eleven years earlier. When their father, Gordon, disappears as well, they are left as wards of their callous grandmother and sour Aunt Vinny until a dispirited Gordon returns seven years later with his new wife, Debbie, a wan substitute for their adored mother. As an omniscient narrator, Isobel can see the past and knows the future, but is not privy to the details of Eliza's disappearance, which forms the tragic secret at the heart of the novel. Like Ruby, the neglected, lonely heroine of *Human Croquet* uses humor to gloss her gloom, making the novel simultaneously heartbreaking and hilarious.

A modern day fairy tale, *Human Croquet* is more magical than *Behind the Scenes*, but also more macabre. Atkinson draws on the menace of the original fairy tales to expose the underside of ordinary life, which features murder, incest, and domestic violence. *Human Croquet* is also more fantastic than its predecessor. As in *Behind the Scenes*, the narrative alternates between past and present, and history repeats itself, but multiple realities and parallel worlds are rendered more explicit through Isobel's time travel. The mutability of time and plasticity of the real makes Isobel an inhabitant of a world in which everything is possible and nothing certain. The novel's enchanting exploration of perception and imagination made it both a number one bestseller and a *New York Times* Notable Book of the Year. As her literary career flourished, Atkinson received the EM Forster Award from the American Academy of Arts and Letters in 1998.

Emotionally Weird (2000), subtitled "A Comic Novel", is the most riotous, lighthearted, and absurdist of Atkinson's books, but one that still raises serious issues and embraces her typical concerns. Sequestered in their dank ancestral home on a bleak island some- where off the West Coast of Scotland, Euphemia Stuart-Murray (Effie) and her mother, Nora, tell each other tales to pass the time and impose order on the chaos of their lives. Effie's stories focus on her experience as a student of English at Dundee University in 1972 and feature a cast of eccentric characters and surreal events. Her narrative is interlaced with excerpts from the various scripts she is writing (an essay on George Eliot, a dissertation on Henry James and a novel for her creative writing class), as well as extracts from the appalling literary efforts of fellow students, which are each presented in a different typeface. Stories proliferate wildly, making *Emotionally Weird* what Alex Clark calls "a carnival of confabula- tion." Nora's more gothic narrative interweaves her daughter's story. Told with greater reluctance and economy, it concerns their ances- tors, family myths, and the enigma of Effie's parentage. Fanciful and flexible stories unfold in a random, giddy manner as the two narrators improvise and revise their tales. The two provisional and apparently inconsequential narratives eventually converge. As they do, secrets are unraveled and mysteries solved, although in the end the tallest story of all turns out to be the truth. *Emotionally Weird* explores the nature and function of storytelling, the boundary be- tween fact and fiction, imagination and reality, and the relationship between language and identity. A novel that probes some challenging philosophical ideas in a gleefully experimental fashion, *Emotionally Weird* received mixed reviews. Nevertheless, its accessibility and sense of fun made it another bestseller.

As well as being an internationally acclaimed novelist, Atkinson is an accomplished dramatist and screenwriter. *Nice* (1996), a stage adaptation of her short story "Inner Balance," was performed in Edinburgh as part of the Traverse Theatre's "Sharp Shorts" series, and she has written a short screenplay called *Karmic Mothers* (1997), based on her prize-winning story of the same title. She is also currently adapting *Behind the Scenes* for television. *Abandonment* (2000), initially conceived as a novel, is her first full-length stage play. It centers on Elizabeth, a recently separated forty-something historian who moves into a dilapidated house haunted by the ghost of a Victorian governess. There she is beset by her adoptive mother, Ina, her sister, Kitty, her best friend, Suzy, the builder, Callum, and her new lover, Alec. Like the novels, the play explores fractious family relationships and the wounds that damaged people inflict on each other. As in *Behind the Scenes*, mother-daughter conflict and sibling rivalry prevail until the characters confront and come to terms with their pain by taking responsibility for it rather than simply blaming their misery on others. As this occurs, tensions are resolved, making reconciliation the keynote of the play's denouement.

The play shares with the novels several thematic and stylistic traits. Scenes set in the present alternate with scenes from the past, which gradually reveal the story of Agnes, the house ghost who bears witness to events in Elizabeth's life. Pregnant by her employer-lover, Agnes is dismissed and then murdered when she threatens to cause a scandal. Abandonment, the source of all the characters' emotional damage, is the motif that unites them. Parallels between Agnes and Elizabeth point to the repetition of the past, an idea reinforced visually on stage by using actors who play characters in the Victorian period to double as their modern day counterparts. Like Ruby's recovery of lost memories in *Behind the Scenes*, the discovery of Agnes' body under the floorboards in the penultimate scene represents the obtrusion of the past on the present. In both works, the past has to be acknowledged before change can occur and a sense of peace prevail. Directed by John Tiffany and first performed as part of the Edinburgh Festival 2000, *Abandonment* won Atkinson considerable praise as a playwright. Writing in *The Times*, Benedict Nightingale declared it a "most promising stage debut" and Michael Billington announced in *The Guardian* that "Atkinson has arrived at theatrical customs with a huge amount to declare."

Atkinson has continued to publish literary short stories and commercial magazine fiction. In Britain, her stories have been read on Radio 4 and appeared in publications such as *Woman's Own, Women's Realm, Good Housekeeping, The Scotsman*, the *Daily Mail*, the *Daily Express*, and the *Daily Telegraph*. With its focus on the quotidian, her short fiction follows in the tradition of Anton Chekhov and Katherine Mansfield, but infuses this tradition with pace and humor. She is currently compiling a collection of stories called *Not the End of the World* while simultaneously working on her fourth novel, *Dogs in Jeopardy*. Developing *Abandonment's* allusions to quantum physics, the plot of *Dogs in Jeopardy* is based on the principles of chaos theory and concerns the multiple ways that chance and coincidence can shape a single life. Having completed the trilogy, Atkinson is keen to "close the gate" on the first three novels and embrace new challenges in the future.

Behind the Scenes, Human Croquet, and *Emotionally Weird* constitute a trilogy in the sense that they all focus on young female protagonists engaged in a quest for identity. To know herself, the heroine must know her past, which makes origins and ancestry crucial to her development. History and memory are key concerns. For Atkinson, who describes herself as pathologically nostalgic, "writing is the act of rescuing the past, even if it's only an imaginary one." Mother-daughter relations are a major theme throughout the trilogy. Atkinson persistently depicts the pain of feeling unmothered or inadequately mothered, as well as the enduring power of the mother-daughter bond. She also dymythifies motherhood by exposing it as a social construct rather than a biological instinct. The family is another focus in her work. Atkinson has made public her view that the conventional nuclear family is a "pernicious" and "destructive" institution. By privileging community over family, she adopts a position that counters Margaret Thatcher's assertion that, "There is no such thing as society. There are individual men and women, and there are families" (p. 10). In response to the demonization of single mothers in the 1980s and 1990s, Atkinson defends single-parent households and is impatient with the piety and sham of the Conservative party's "back to basics" campaign, which presented the family as the center of morality and celebrated "Victorian family values." In Atkinson's fictional world, the traditional family unit is unhealthy or abusive, and this prompts the heroines' search for home. In *Behind the Scenes*, Ruby makes her home in Scotland and Scotland is significant throughout Atkinson's oeuvre either in terms of setting or ancestry. However, the central significance of Scotland lies in its resistance to English hegemony. Reflecting on her decision to move to Scotland, Atkinson has said: "there's something lacking in England, something about being English that's far from fulfilling." This sense of dissatisfaction with Englishness finds expression in her fiction through the deconstruction of dominant myths and images of England and English national identity.

Atkinson's work is also distinguished by a number of idiosyncratic concerns, namely a preoccupation with death, genes, and dogs. A staggering number of characters die in *Behind the Scenes*, although rarely do the dead disappear for good. A fascination with death has lead her to fantasize about her own funeral and she has a file in her cabinet called "What to do when I'm dead." She also wants to be buried with a Victorian grave bell so that she can be rescued if she is not really dead. A lapsed Quaker, Atkinson does not believe in God or an afterlife: "meaning isn't something that has to be attached to another world or another realm, but exists within us, here and now. And it's our task to discover it within ourselves, and within the world, while we're still here." Atkinson's interest in genes relates to the more general theme of identity, and raises the issue of whether identity is the product of nature or nurture. Several characters account for their personality or the pattern of their lives in terms of genetic predisposition. However, because this biological explanation overlooks the social factors that shape the characters' experience, it is invariably inadequate or unconvincing. Dogs, often more reliable, faithful, and unconditionally loving than humans, provide the emotional sustenance missing from several characters' lives, and many of the most poignant scenes in Atkinson's fiction feature the death of dogs. Her obsession with dogs has inspired a series of "doggy" short stories, including "This Dog's Life" and "A Partner for Life."

Atkinson's novels are similar not only in terms of subject but also style. A salient feature of her writing is its comic tone. She has the ability to be both wildly witty and deeply touching. Her hallmark wry humor, which combines comedy with pathos, is accompanied by an irrepressible imagination. A startlingly original and endlessly inventive writer, her restless ingenuity gives her work a playful, quirky quality. She writes with lustre and panache, her agile, exuberant prose alive with linguistic virtuosity. The energy of the prose comes in good part from pace. She hatches and dispatches a vast cast of characters with velocity, and packs an intricate plot with scores of twists and turns, making the texts fast and full. These characteristics meld together within a meticulously crafted, complex structure. Always attentive to the form of the novel, Atkinson stresses the importance of craft: "writing doesn't spring from the soul — it's a work of art." ·

Atkinson's anarchic style stems from an irreverence for convention. She subverts traditional assumptions about the novel and toys with the principles of classic realism through disrupted chronology, a fragmented, non-linear structure, and a disregard for accurate, detailed description. For example, readers never learn what Ruby Lennox looks like. Her self-conscious narrators become increasingly intrusive throughout the trilogy but Ruby, Isobel, and Effie all flaunt their control of the narrative and draw attention to the act of story-telling. The novels stress artifice and advertise an awareness of their fictional status. For Atkinson, "books aren't about things, they *are* things," and she stresses the materiality of the text through unusual typographic features: footnotes in *Behind the Scenes*, large font in *Human Croquet*, a semi-black page in *Emotionally Weird*. Whereas realism treats language as a transparent medium of communication, Atkinson draws attention to language and underlines the text's status as a linguistic construct. She confounds literary categories by blending a range of non-realist genres: the picaresque, romance, melodrama, farce, fantasy, and fairy tale. While all of these features are evident in *Behind the Scenes*, they become more marked throughout the trilogy and most explicit in *Emotionally Weird* — the most self-reflexive and self-referential of the three novels — where they are pursued to the extent of parody.

Another dominant feature of Atkinson's writing is intertextuality or bricolage. Direct references and allusions to other literary texts abound. Among other texts, *Behind the Scenes* invokes Henry James' *The Turn of the Screw* (p. 265), Charles Dickens' *Great Expectations* (p. 283), Bram Stoker's *Dracula* (p. 290), Emily Bronte's *Wuthering Heights* (p. 318), Daphne Du Maurier's *Rebecca* (p. 353), and John

Webster's *The Duchess of Malfi* (p. 360). (Page references are to the British edition of the novel.) Intertextuality has several functions. First, because *Behind the Scenes* pilfers from sources ranging from Shakespeare to *The Sound of Music*, it collapses the boundary between elite and popular culture and challenges traditional hierarchies of value. Second, like typographic eccentricity and verbal artifice, it advertises the constructedness of the text by emphasizing that it is composed of fragments of other texts. Third, Atkinson's use of intertextuality brings together theme and form by creating a sense of the persistence or repetition of the past, a motif that runs throughout the trilogy. However, because past literary works are either consciously revised or changed simply by being placed in a different context, intertextuality enacts the process of repetition and change — a quintessential theme in *Behind the Scenes*. Last, by revising the texts she invokes, Atkinson challenges their authority. As Hilary Mantel observes, "She is not so much standing on the shoulders of giants, as darting between their legs and waving her own agenda — and talking all the time, with a voice that is entirely her own."

While Atkinson draws on a wide variety of sources in her writing, the texts she returns to most persistently are fairy tales; specifically, Lewis Carroll's *Alice's Adventures in Wonderland* (1865) and *Through the Looking Glass* (1871). With no siblings, Atkinson's chief companions in childhood were books, and she read voraciously. Fairy tales had a profound and lasting impact on her imagination. The trilogy contains countless allusions to classical fairy tales and repeatedly employs the fairy tale motifs of quest and test. The central protagonists all identify with fairy tale figures and accept fairy tales as true, as Atkinson did herself until well into her thirties. According to Jack Zipes, the seductive appeal of fairy tales lies in their utopian impulse and the motif of metamorphosis. In his numerous books on fairy tales, including *Breaking the Magic Spell: Radical Theories of Folk and Fairy Tales* (1979) and *When Dreams*

Come True: Classical Fairy Tales and Their Tradition (1999), Zipes observes that many fairy tales focus on family conflict and most dramatize triumph over adversity. The tales feature protagonists who survive in a hostile environment and overcome oppression by taking control of their own fate. Through the magical transformation of self and situation, fairy tales thus present the possibility of leading a happier life in a better world.

The fairy tale figure with whom Atkinson's protagonists identify most strongly is Carroll's Alice. As a child, her favorite book was *Alice's Adventures in Wonderland*, which she re-read every week between the ages of five and ten. As a lonely, gloomy, only child, Atkinson found solace in fiction and nurtured her own fantasy worlds. She took comfort in Carroll's acceptance of the absurd, found the insanity of the Alice stories appealing, and reveled in their departure from common sense. Enthralled by the idea of alternative worlds, she relished Alice's ability to slip in and out of different realities. Both *Alice's Adventures in Wonderland* and its successor, *Through the Looking Glass*, became a major influence on her work and, in many ways, the trilogy is based on the Alice stories. Carroll and Atkinson both construct narratives of personal development and self-discovery that feature young heroines making the transition from childhood to adulthood. Like Alice, Atkinson's heroines find themselves isolated in a strange, mysterious, sometimes sinister world but become gradually stronger and more self-possessed. Like Carroll, Atkinson is alert to the perils of childhood and presents the behavior of adults as bewildering or threatening. Both writers delight in the slipperiness of language and question what is real.

Behind the Scenes owes a clear debt to the Alice stories. Ruby remarks that she feels like Alice on several occasions, her descent through the Lost Property Cupboard echoes Alice's fall down the rabbit hole, and during a session with Dr. Herzmark she almost drowns, like Alice, in her own pool of tears. Human croquet, the game that Bunty's Sunday School play on the beach in footnote six (also the title of Atkinson's second novel), echoes the croquet game Alice plays using hedgehogs as balls, flamingoes as mallets, and playing card guards as hoops. Bunty, Ruby's apparently heartless mother, is reminiscent of the imperious Queen of Hearts although her smile belongs to the Cheshire cat, and Daisy and Rose resemble Tweedledum and Tweedledee. Alice, Ruby's great-grandmother, enters "her own private wonderland" when she has an out of body experience that takes her away from the "real" world (p. 34).

Part of the appeal of the Alice stories lies in their subversive power. While the increasing commercialization of fairy tales has reduced them to agents of socialization that reinforce the status quo by confirming dominant ideologies of gender and class, Lewis Carroll is exceptional in his use of fantasy to question rather than confirm existing social relations. Like L. Frank Baum's *The Wizard of Oz* (1900), another significant influence, Carroll's narratives contain an unconventional heroine who defies traditional gender stereotypes endorsed in contemporary versions of most fairy tales. Both Alice and Dorothy are independent and active agents who demonstrate courage and initiative, and become increasingly bold and self-assertive. Atkinson affirms such qualities in her heroines while debunking romantic myths propagated by modern day fairy tales, particularly the myth that marriage results in happiness ever after. In *Behind the Scenes*, the story of Alice, who is seduced by the "rococo exotica of Monsieur Armand's vowels" (p. 341), warns of the perils of romance. After leaving her children to elope with the itinerant French photographer, "she lived long enough to regret more or less everything" (p. 344). Atkinson presents romance as either dangerous or ridiculous. Romance is undercut by the figure of Bernard Belling, Bunty's "Prince Valiant," who has "a plumbing supplies business somewhere in the nether-regions of Black Swinegate" (p. 316), and the revelation that Ruby's proposal of marriage from Gian-Carlo Benedetti is not the result of destiny, as she wants to believe, but the threat of deportment.

Atkinson's other primary influence is Laurence Sterne's *Tristram Shandy* (1759–67). In *Behind the Scenes*, Ruby claims that Sterne is one of the ghosts living Above the Shop: "You can hear them if you listen hard. . . . the *scratch-scratch* of the Reverend Sterne's quill" (p. 10). However, Sterne haunts the whole novel, not just Ruby's house. There are a significant number of parallels between the two texts. *Tristram Shandy* and *Behind the Scenes* are both picaresques, novels that relate a journey or quest and possess episodic plots that feature farcical events. Both texts are fictional autobiographies set in York, open with the narrator's description of his/her own conception and birth, and digress from the main narrative to relate aspects of family history. Both feature fractured narratives that jump backwards and forwards in time. Tristram and Ruby are both first person narrators who claim an omniscience that is undermined by their subjective and selective point of view. Just as *Tristram Shandy* contains self-involved characters who are blinded by their personal obsessions or "hobbyhorses," so Ruby's pain and self-pity prevent her from seeing situations clearly. Like Ruby, Tristram draws attention to the act of storytelling as he self-consciously reflects on the process of literary creation, and, like Atkinson, Sterne highlights the book's status as a material object by inserting blank, black and marbled pages, and using different fonts and graphics. Sterne takes Cervantes' *Don Quixote* (1547–1616) as his model, and the influence of Cervantes (regarded by many as the single most important progenitor of the modern novel) runs through Sterne to Atkinson, who both explore the relationship between illusion and reality through quixotic central characters. Sterne's presence looms large in *Behind the Scenes* and *Tristram Shandy* remains an intertextual touchstone throughout the trilogy as Atkinson continues to revive and rework the novelistic conventions of the eighteenth century.

Atkinson's ludic influences extend from Sterne and Carroll to a number of postmodern American writers. Donald Barthelme and Robert Coover prompted her to look at writing in a new way and made her want to be a writer. However, her favorite writer is Kurt Vonnegut, a master of the tall tale, who, like Atkinson, began his literary career writing short stories for magazines. Attracted to the fearlessness and playfulness of postmodern fiction, Atkinson made postmodern short stories the subject of her doctoral thesis, a study that focused on the American writers John Barth, Steve Katz, and Ronald Sukenick, as well as Barthelme and Coover. Although different in significant ways, the work of these highly experimental and humorous postmodern writers shares several dominant characteristics: a radical departure from realist norms, metafictionality, an emphasis on form over content, non-linearity, and a fragmentary style based on the principles of collage, free association, and juxtaposition. They seek to challenge established forms of representation by reinventing conventional literary codes. They also share an interest in similar subjects: epistemological uncertainty, the fictive nature of history, the interconnection of public and private stories, the function of myth, the slipperiness of language, the complexities of reality, the multiplicity of meaning, and the impossibility of establishing a coherent perspective on the world. The influence of postmodern writers is palpable in Atkinson's fiction, although in some ways her work is quite different. Like postmodern writers, she insists that writing has no rules and presents reality as a linguistic and discursive construct. However, Atkinson never loses sight of the material and psychological conditions of female oppression. Furthermore, by presenting women as agents of change, she refuses a postmodern scepticism of the Enlightenment faith in emancipation and historical progress.

Other influences are reflected in the literary Top Ten Atkinson compiled for *The Guardian*:

1. *The Great Gatsby* by F. Scott Fitzgerald
2. *Slaughterhouse Five* by Kurt Vonnegut
3. *Pride and Prejudice* by Jane Austen
4. *Just William* by Richman Crompton
5. *What Maisie Knew* by Henry James
6. *Pricksongs and Descants* by Robert Coover/*Collected Stories* by Donald Barthelme
7. *Alice in Wonderland* and *Through the Looking Glass* by Lewis Carroll
8. *Lolita* by Vladimir Nabokov
9. *Middlemarch* by George Eliot
10. *Huckleberry Finn* by Mark Twain
11. *The Good Soldier* by Ford Maddox Ford

The list demonstrates Atkinson's eclectic literary taste as well as her characteristically cheeky defiance of limits (she gives eleven choices but actually squeezes thirteen books into what is supposed to be a Top Ten). It reflects her love of fantasy (Carroll), classic realism (Austen, Eliot), romance (Twain, Fitzgerald), and postmodernism (Vonnegut, Barthelme, Coover); her admiration of highbrow literature (Nabokov, James, Ford) and popular fiction (Twain, Crompton). Atkinson's writing is akin to that of the writers she admires in a number of ways. Like the authors of many classic American novels such as *Huckleberry Finn*, *The Great Gatsby*, and *Lolita*, she favors first person narration. Like Austen and Eliot she is interested in narratives of female development and women's struggle for selfhood in a patriarchal world. Her novels, like theirs, contain a number of motherless heroines. Like Crompton and James, she is concerned with the experience of childhood and portrays the world from a child's point of view. Like James, Ford, and Nabokov she exploits unreliable narration and encourages readers to question the narrator's limited and romanticized worldview. Atkinson shares Nabokov's wit, love of language games, and a tendency to kill off characters suddenly. Like the modernists James and Ford, her exploration of memory and the mind's ability to deceive itself often makes what is not said the most important thing on the page. Like Twain, she writes literary fiction that has popular appeal and bridges the gap between the academy and the market place. The quality that Atkinson values most in the writers she admires is their ability to invest structure with emotion, to render emotion through structure, and not sacrifice one for the other. For her, Vonnegut's *Slaughterhouse Five* represents the best example of the indivisibility of the two. As her oversized selection indicates, Atkinson's literary preferences exceed the list. She also respects Douglas Coupland (another fan of Vonnegut) and enjoys reading Anne Tyler, Alice Hoffman, Margaret Atwood, Barbara Kingsolver, Jane Hamilton, and Jane Smiley. Atkinson's reading and interest in postmodernism, which is international in character and at odds with what Antony Easthope regards as the dominant British tradition of empiricism, are indicative of the way in which she situates herself outside of British literary tradition. Although she shares a self-conscious awareness of form with authors such as Jeanette Winterson, Salman Rushdie, and Alasdair Gray, she is—particularly in *Behind the Scenes*—more subtle in her deployment of frame-breaking devices, and stands aloof from contemporary British fiction.

Although she does not define herself as a "woman writer," there are certain affinities between Atkinson and a range of other international contemporary women writers who recuperate and celebrate the marginalized and traditionally feminine literary form of fairy tales while simultaneously revising the male-dominated literary tradition they inherit. For example, Atkinson appropriates the picaresque, a form traditionally championed by male writers and fashioned for a male hero, as *Tristram Shandy* shows. *Tristram Shandy*, in fact, exemplifies a tradition that is both patriarchal and phallocentric: it focuses on a father-son relationship and contains a plethora of penis jokes that revolve around Tristram's accidental circumcision and Uncle Toby's groin injury. Whereas Sterne focuses on filial relations, *Behind the Scenes* concerns the relationship between mothers and daughters, and Atkinson's allusions to *Tristram Shandy* thus draw attention to the occlusion of the mother while making space for her in fiction. Despite affinities with other women writers who resist and revise a patriarchal literary tradition, Atkinson refuses the labels "women's writing" and "feminist fiction" for her work. This may seem surprising for a woman who was a founding member of the Women's Liberation group at Dundee University and "embraced the base" at Greenham Common Women's Peace Camp. (She was also once arrested during a protest at Upper Heyford American air base on what she describes as the "disappointingly pedestrian charge" of obstructing a public highway.) However, Atkinson rejects these labels for the same reason that she became involved in feminist activism: to contest patriarchy. Terms like "women's writing" can be problematic because they imply that writing is the province of men and that female authors are an exception or aberration. Such terms threaten to ghettoize writing by women because of the assumption that books *by* or *about* women are books *for* women. While novels about men are understood to be novels about a universal human condition, texts that focus on female experience tend to be considered more narrow and dismissed as "chick lit" (a literary equivalent of the cinematic "chick flick"). The label "feminist fiction" is equally problematic as it implies both fiction for feminists and a political manifesto. To assume that a writer functions as a mouthpiece for a particular ideology is demeaning because it denies their creativity and originality. While Atkinson's work is woman-centerd, she does not write for a specific audience and her texts hold significance for male and female readers alike. So, although Atkinson rejects the labels "women's writing" and "feminist fiction" she does so out of feminist sympathies and in order to challenge patriarchal assumptions that undermine women's literary achievements. As the next chapter will show, feminism also shapes her fiction in significant ways.

2

The Novel

Behind the Scenes is primarily a "bildungsroman," a novel of formation that follows the protagonist's passage from childhood to maturity, often passing through crisis en route to self-recognition. While Ruby's quest for selfhood is central, the story of her growth from womb to womanhood encompasses themes that link the personal and the political. Through an exploration of subjects such as memory, history, mother-daughter relations, Englishness and home, Atkinson connects private and public realms of experience in a manner that gives her work impressive scope. This chapter will discuss the text's major themes but, because many of its themes are reflected in or conveyed through form, will begin with a consideration of narrative technique.

NARRATION AND POINT OF VIEW

Behind the Scenes is narrated by its central character whose sassy voice dominates and defines the novel. The brio of Ruby's narrative derives in good part from its doubleness. In a manner reminiscent of Henry James' *What Maisie Knew* (1897), the novel presents a child's viewpoint in an adult voice. As her language demonstrates, Ruby speaks as a child, but not like a child. She draws attention to her restricted word power, and ironically boasts "an astonishingly mature vocabulary list of ten words," yet simultaneously uses sophisticated terms such as "nomenclature" (p. 86). Ruby's voice also implies knowledge beyond her years. Erudite, articulate and informed, her narrative is dotted with reference to things such as a "Sisyphean nightmare" and "Strindbergian gloom" (p. 25; p. 118). Pondering her family's habit of shouting "Shop!", the foetal Ruby wonders, "Are they addressing the shop in the vocative case (O Shop!) or naming it in the nominative?" (p. 17). Atkinson thus makes explicit a narrative feature that, as Nicola King points out, most (fictional) autobiographies tend to elide: "The 'I' who speaks is not the 'I' who is spoken of" (p. 19). A foetus-infant-girl who speaks like a grown-up in a style that is simultaneously cynical and naïve, Ruby embodies innocence and experience combined. When Patricia informs Ruby that she is about to lose her virginity, Ruby offers to help her look for it. Yet a worldly-wise eight-year-old Ruby also sympathizes with Patricia's adolescent efforts at femininity: "Sometimes it's hard to be a woman" (p. 198). In fact, by the time she is born, Ruby is already world-weary: "Well, there you go — nothing surprises me anymore" (p. 40).

The doubleness of Ruby's voice is marked by the use of parenthesis, which often separates the voice of innocence and experience and indicates a double perspective: "So I come to Scotland a second time and if I knew how long I was going to stay (for ever) I expect I would do some things differently — bring more clothes, for example" (p. 353). The remark Ruby makes about the spiritualist meeting she attends with Auntie Babs offers another example: "I suppose I won't be spoken to because I don't know anybody who's dead (how wrong I am)" (p. 119). Ruby narrates her life story in the present tense and seems to be relating events as they occur: "Hang on a minute — there's something missing from this inventory, isn't there?" (p. 250). However, a sense of immediacy is accompanied by a sense of distance. This is underlined when Ruby places her experience in a historical context, and thereby indicates an awareness of social change: "George stubs out his cigarette and makes a kind of snorting noise in his throat and settles back into his chair to watch Bunty making his cup of tea (well, this *is* 1959)" (p. 176). The discrepancy between youth and maturity (Ruby's age and voice) is not merely a comic device but an example of the way in which Atkinson integrates subject and style and uses form and content to reflect each other. Ruby does not recognize that she had a twin sister until Dr. Herzmark helps her to recover repressed memories of Pearl's death. By creating the impression that there are two Rubys, the duality of her voice anticipates this revelation and reflects her unacknowledged status as a twin. Ruby is a "jewel twin" who has a dual voice and vision (p. 330).

The duality of Ruby's voice stems from her unusual status as a first person "omniscient" narrator. She tells her story from her own point of view but also enjoys daimonic powers associated with a third person omniscient narrator who typically stands outside the action and describes events in a detached, impersonal, objective manner. As first and third person forms of narration are diametrically opposed, a first person omniscient narrator is an oxymoron. Yet, in a manner reminiscent of *Tristram Shandy*, Atkinson artfully combines first and third person narrative techniques by making Ruby the speaking "I" who narrates events from her own perspective while (apparently) endowing her with a god-like power to see and know all. She knows, for example, even before she is born, that her father is having an affair and is aware of what is happening to other characters, like Uncle Ted who is "in the Merchant Navy and is being tossed on the South China Seas at this moment" (p. 25). She is cognizant of events that occured before her conception and pays witness to the world from Bunty's womb. If Ruby sees what has gone before she also sees what is yet to come and frequently alludes to future events such as Gillian's death, the pet shop fire and the trip that she and Bunty undertake to Australia.

Ruby's omniscience and maturity of voice lend her narrative an air of authority, which is compounded by the use of inventories and footnotes. Ruby's various lists (of relatives, vocabulary, conversation topics, school uniform) create the impression of accuracy and relia-bility. As footnotes are a form of discourse usually associated with non-fictional texts and typically offer evidence to verify an argument, they also create the impression that Ruby's narrative is trustworthy. At the same time, her credibility is called into question by the first person point of view, which renders her narrative partial and subjective. Because Ruby's unreliability stems not from dishon-esty but human fallibility (deceptions of memory, private interests and preoccupations, and misinterpretation of events), it offers a realistic reflection of human subjectivity. As Salman Rushdie, with whom Atkinson shares an interest in unreliable narration, points out:

human beings do not perceive things whole; we are not gods but wounded creatures, cracked lenses, capable only of fractured perceptions. Partial beings, in all senses of the phrase. Meaning is a shaky edifice we build out of scraps, dogmas, childhood injuries, newspaper articles, chance remarks, old films, small victories, people hated, people loved. (*Imaginary Home-lands*, p. 12)

In *Behind the Scenes*, unreliable narration reveals the workings of Ruby's mind and provides valuable insights into her psychology. Her unreliability is indicated in three main ways. First, it is signaled by gaps in the narrative. The largest and, viewed retrospectively, most obvious gap relates to Pearl. Ruby not only represses her memory of Pearl's death but also suppresses details that have uncomfortable associations. The most explicit gap occurs as Ruby suddenly breaks off her narrative when Bernard Belling accuses her of killing Pearl. She also misses out William in her list of relatives and, although she mentions that Babs is in hospital and later makes reference to her funeral, neglects to mention her aunt's actual death. The omission of William (Ada's twin, who dies aged three months) mirrors Ruby's denial of her own twin and the occlusion of Babs' death is indicative of the difficulties she has dealing with loss. Although Pearl's death remains unregistered until near the end of the novel, Ruby draws attention to her unreliable memory throughout. After her fight with Gillian over the Mobo horse, she admits, "The rest of the day is a bit of a blur" (p. 88). She also confesses that she cannot recall how she gets to Dewsbury and admits to having forgotten what happened to her father's ashes. If Ruby withholds information, there is also a suggestion that she is simply not in full possession of the facts. She admits to a limited perspective when she confesses, "I know nothing" (p. 227; p. 353). Even when Ruby delivers the facts, she cannot always be relied upon to highlight their significance, as when she neglects to point out that George's mistress (Mrs. Doreen Collier) and Edmund's lover (Doreen O'Doherty) are the same woman. It is left to the reader to piece together various clues (both women are Belfast-born nurses who give up babies for adoption) and to surmise, therefore, that Sister Blake is Edmund's daughter and Ruby's relative. By encouraging the reader to make these connections, Atkinson transforms the reader's role from passive consumer to active participant in the construction of meaning.

The second way in which Ruby's unreliability is conveyed is through her hyperactive imagination. Like Nabokov's Humbert

Humbert in *Lolita* (1955) and Charles Kinbote in *Pale Fire* (1962), she confuses imagination and reality (although whereas one is a pedophile desperate to defend his life and the other a demented literary critic, Ruby is an ordinary child). Ruby imagines crocodiles, dragons, and nameless things living under the camp bed and wolves on the stairs at Aunt Babs' house and, irrepressibly quixotic, sees her life through a fairy tale lens. She refers to Above the Shop as Bunty's "kingdom" (p. 173), and describes the garden hedge that separates their house from that of the Ropers as a "battlement between our suburban castles" (p. 246). Fantasizing about her wedding, she states: "My antique lace dress will fall in drifts of snow and it will be garlanded and swagged with rosebuds as if the little birds who helped Cinderella dress for the ball had flown round and round me, nipping and tucking and pinning" (p. 286). Such a romantic sensibility renders the reliability of her narrative dubious.

Ruby's predilection for melodrama suggests a tendency to embroider events described: "A cold wind suddenly blows as the kitchen door is flung open dramatically and a dark shadow falls across the yard. The shadow is not merely dark, it contains the squid-inky evil of hatred, jealousy and murderous inclinations—yes, it's our Gillian!" (p. 87). Hyperbole likewise demonstrates her habit of exaggeration. Learning to read *Puppies and Kittens*, she declares, "I am powerful! I have the key to the Temple of Knowledge and there's no stopping me" (p. 125). Ruby's fixation with fantasy could be dismissed as a childish preoccupation, but her flights of fancy persist into adulthood. After Bunty's funeral, Ruby and Patricia visit the tearoom that was once their home, and Ruby imagines a Roman army marching through the streets of York. As Ruby presents fantasy as reality, the reader is left to surmise that she is imagining the scene as reality intrudes—"at that moment a waitress drops a jug full of milk and the Ninth Legion is reduced to a fading echo of footfalls" — and Patricia rouses Ruby from her daydream: "Ruby, Ruby!" Patricia gives me a little shake. "Ruby, what are you staring at? Come on, it's time to go" (p. 379).

Third, unreliability is denoted by misinterpretation. Kathleen Wall has shown that unreliable narration can stem not just from the narrator's inaccurate presentation of scenes witnessed but by a conflict between the narrator's commentary and evidence in the scene commented upon. Ruby's judgements are frequently at odds with the scenes she describes. On holiday in Scotland, she refers to losing the baby-David as a "minor distraction" (p. 260), and after Mrs. Roper is dramatically rushed to hospital, reports that the cause of her pain was "only" appendicitis which "isn't that bad" (p. 265), even though she acknowledges that appendicitis can be fatal. Like Nabokov's Humbert and Kinbote, her interpretative powers are skewed by solipsism. Shortly after her conception, Ruby assumes that the dawn chorus is "heralding my own arrival" and deludes herself that the birds in the park are "miniature angels of the Annunciation, avian Gabriels, come to shout my arrival! Alleluia!" (p. 11; p. 18). A discrepancy between the events Ruby relates and her evaluation of them indicates a conflict between internal and external reality. Because her narrative privileges interiority, her interpretation of facts is often colored by feelings. An example of this occurs when Bunty and George return home after a week's absence following Gillian's death. Feeling neglected, Ruby accuses her parents of abrogating parental responsibility and wonders why they went to stay with Clifford and Gladys: "perhaps they wanted to be looked after or perhaps (less likely) they wanted to protect us from the aftermath of the tragedy" (pp. 188–9). The probability that the view Ruby rejects is more accurate than the one she endorses — "Bunty didn't care" (p. 185) — is suggested by a parallel with her father's strategy for deception (although whereas George deliberately seeks to deceive others, Ruby's narrative ruse is the product of self-deception). When George defensively asks Bunty "what do you think I'm doing—meeting another woman for a riotous night on the tiles?" (p. 25), he speaks the truth in order to deny it. Ruby's rebuttal thus ironically endorses the very interpretation she seeks to deny, and encourages a skeptical reconsideration of her narrative.

Wall points out that most unreliable narrators are, in some ways, actually quite reliable and, while Ruby's interpretation of certain scenes seems dubious, there is little reason to doubt the details of the scenes she describes. Reading *Behind the Scenes* does not, therefore, involve reading between the lines—the means by which Wayne Booth argues unreliability is detected in *The Rhetoric of Fiction* (1961)—because Ruby's account is largely correct, as well as emotionally honest. By making Ruby simultaneously reliable and unreliable, Atkinson undermines the distinction between two apparently mutually exclusive forms of narration and deconstructs an opposition predicated on the assumption that it is possible to tell the truth.

The novel persistently problematizes the concept of truth. The children's response to Aunt Babs' "illness" suggests that truth is not absolute but arbitrary and contingent. Even though they know that their mother has not gone to nurse Babs as George tells them when she disappears, they begin to discuss their aunt's "illness" as if it were real: "This last fact has been stated so many times over the last twenty-four hours that we're beginning to believe it's the truth" (p. 153). Atkinson's subversion of narrative convention likewise undermines the notion of absolute truth. Whereas unreliable first person narration stresses subjectivity of point of view, unreliable first person "omniscient" narration takes this one step further by showing that omniscience is a pretense and an illusion. The deceptions enacted by Ruby's tricksy narrative illustrate that all points of view are inevitably incomplete, subjective, and biased, even those (perhaps especially those) that appear or purport to be reliable. In this way, the novel stresses the impossibility of absolute knowledge and the provisional nature of truth.

In *The Art of Fiction* (1992), David Lodge comments that an unreliable "omniscient" narrator "could only occur in a very deviant, experimental text" (p. 154). Atkinson deviates from realism using a number of experimental literary techniques. While realism presupposes a pre-existing reality and common phenomenal world, *Behind the Scenes* suggests that reality is not stable, singular and self-evident. After the holiday in Whitby, Ruby notes the unreal nature of reality: "The holiday rapidly takes on the quality of myth — faded and tantalizingly beyond recall—as if it had happened to children in a story rather than us. . . . For a while we talked about Auntie Doreen amongst ourselves but, by and by, she grew as unreal as Mary Poppins herself" (p. 164). On holiday in Scotland, reality takes on the glow of hallucination when Ruby sees a stag: "I don't even bother prodding Patricia to tell her about him, because I know I must be dreaming" (p. 266). Ruby also senses alternative realities: "Somewhere just beyond the mist, there's our real Scottish holiday — and perhaps all the other holidays we never had as well" (p. 266). The idea of alternative realities is developed by allusions to *The Wizard of Oz*, which align Ruby with Dorothy, the character who crosses between the parallel worlds of Kansas and Oz. The house ghosts who, like Dorothy, cross between different ontological realms, likewise point to parallel worlds. Like a romance, a genre that privileges what is possible over what is probable, Ruby's narrative questions what is real by taking the reader into what Nathaniel Hawthorne calls a territory "somewhere between the real world and fairy-land, where the Actual and the Imaginary may meet, and each imbue itself with the nature of the other" (Chase, pp. 18–19).

The photograph of Alice that deceptively hides her pregnancy and features a *"trompe-l'oeil* balustraded staircase" indicates that mimetic art does not guarantee an accurate and reliable reflection of reality and shows that appearances can be deceptive (p. 27). The novel also questions language's ability to reflect reality by exposing a gap between signifier and signified, that is, by demonstrating that there is no direct relationship between word and world. "Above the Shop," for example, is not actually above the shop (p. 10). Shattering a mimetic theory of art, the novel suggests that literature constructs rather than reflects reality. Ruby renders transparent the process of fictionalization by visibly inventing details such as the names of the two men in the park "who we will call Bert and Alf" (p. 18), making reference to aspects of fiction such as "plot" (p. 183), and emphasizing the act of storytelling: "This is the story of my grandmother's continually thwarted attempts to get married" (p. 45). She also addresses the reader: "My absent father, in case you're wondering, is in the Dog and Hare in Doncaster" (p. 40). Like her use of first person "omniscient" narration, Atkinson's postmodern narrative strategies expose the limits and illusions of realism, and reflect a presiding concern with questions about how we know, and the extent to which we can know, the world around us.

MEMORY

Behind the Scenes registers a powerful interest in memory. For Ruby, memory is crucial to the self-knowledge required for personal development. However, the subject of memory also corresponds to broader political concerns about the recollection of trauma and collective amnesia. Like South Africa's truth and reconciliation commission, African American demands for reparations for slavery, and Holocaust Memorial Day, *Behind the Scenes* stresses the importance of not forgetting the past and shares Rabbi Baal Shem Tov's conviction that remembrance is the secret of redemption.

Ruby has a bad memory in the dual sense that her memories are unpleasant and her memory is unreliable. She represses Pearl's death in order to protect herself from pain and stores traumatic memories in her Lost Property Cupboard, a metaphor for the unconscious mind. A desire to block things out is epitomised by her longing for "earlids" (p. 248). The doubleness of Ruby's narrative voice thus reflects not only her status as a twin but also the conflict between her conscious and unconscious mind. Although she attempts to expel Pearl from consciousness, repressed memories persistently threaten to return, as when Ruby spells out Pearl's name on a ouija-board (p. 124). Water, in particular, triggers Ruby's unconscious memory of the pond where Pearl drowns. Looking at the River Ouse, she finds "a curious feeling rises up inside me, a feeling of something long forgotten" (p. 227), and feels uneasy by the loch in Scotland because "It reminds me of something, but what?" (p. 260). Ruby's preoccupation with water is also reflected in the Latin inscription at the bottom of her metaphysical Lost Property Cupboard: "Deinde ipsa, virum suum complexa, in mare se deiecit" (p. 323). The quotation is taken from Livy's *History of Rome*, an extract of which Ruby is expected to translate in the Latin examination she walks out of just after Bernard Belling accuses her of killing her sister and just prior to her suicide attempt. The quoted words ("And having embraced her husband, she sprang into the sea," taken from 40.4) relate to Theoxena who, choosing death over enslavement to a tyrannical king, throws her sons into the sea before committing suicide. Although Ruby later remembers that Pearl slips into the duck pond, Gillian leads the family to believe that Ruby pushed her. A trace of memories she cannot quite recall in conjunction with Belling's accusation thus trigger Ruby's unconscious identification with Theoxena, who not only drowned members of her family and committed suicide but also had a mother called Berenice.

Ruby employs humor, as well as amnesia, as a means of self-protection and her wit, like her fear of water, can be read as a symptom of repression. Her cheery account of catastrophe and flippant treatment of events that are far from funny create a marked discrepancy between subject and style. From her exuberant opening words "I exist!" (p. 9), Ruby adopts a brisk and breezy style that conceals her growing disappointment behind a blithe façade. As tragedy ensues, she deploys humor as a defense against trauma and masks her melancholy with mirth. Nevertheless, Ruby's underlying sadness finds an oblique outlet in ironic expressions of pity: "Poor cat" (p. 17); "Poor Queen" (p. 86); "Poor York" (p. 103); "Poor Elvis" (p. 231).

While humor makes life easier to bear, *Behind the Scenes* suggests that levity cannot function as a successful long-term strategy for survival in the face of trauma. The novel stresses the dangers of repression and denial. Bunty, for example, has an "unhealed part of her soul" because she remains traumatised by an experience she has been unable to resolve (p. 333). Haunted by the distress of missing the train for the Sunday School outing as a child, Bunty is condemned to relive her ordeal, as her journey to the nursing home demonstrates: "She has already had a fit of near-hysteria as we crawled through York's permanently bottle-necked traffic, under the delusion that we were hopelessly late for a train we were trying to catch, and as we drive past the station and leave it behind she sets up a formidable wail" (p. 370). As monitor of the school lost property cupboard, Ruby recognizes that "There are fearsome consequences for children who do not reclaim their property" (p. 321), and her reluctance to reclaim lost memories indeed has destructive results: a persistent sense of "Unnamed Dread" (p. 126), sleepwalking, panic attacks, depression. Ruby's attempted suicide demonstrates that repression is potentially fatal and emphasizes that she must face the past in order to have a future.

The importance of remembering the past is signified by the color blue, "the colour of memory" (p. 332), and the recurring motif of forget-me-knots which decorate Alice's tea set, grow in Tom's field and describe the color of Albert's and Edmund's eyes, as well as the sky in which Alice floats during her out of body experience and the Scottish sea that triggers Ruby's panic attack. After her suicide attempt, Dr. Herzmark helps Ruby to recover repressed memories by returning her to the scene of trauma in a safe environment: the moment when Pearl drowns in the duck pond at Mabel and Tom's farm. The title of the novel brings the significance of "scenes" into focus and, as the introduction to Alice's story suggests, Ruby perceives memory as a series of scenes that are transcribed into language: "Picture the scene—" (p. 29). Atkinson exploits the ambiguity of language by also using "scene" to indicate a dramatic event, as when Bunty prepares for a "scene" with Gillian or Ruby comments, "I have had a terrible scene with Mr. Belling" (p. 19; p. 323). The word "scene" thus simultaneously suggests the act of remembrance Ruby must undertake and the trauma of the past she must recall. As Ruby recovers her memory, healing is suggested by the desire to move memories of Pearl from the Lost Property Cupboard to her metaphysical bottom drawer. Whereas one holds items lost in the past, the other stores them safely for the future. When Kathleen starts to collect household items in preparation for marriage, Ruby wonders what she would put in her own bottom drawer, and her recovered memories provide an answer: "I have been to the world's end and back and now I know what I would put in my bottom drawer. I would put my sisters" (p. 338).

Behind the Scenes suggests that memory works on a collective as well as an individual level. The transgenerational nature of memory is epitomized by Ruby's "end of the world" dream (p. 211). As the dream contains details of the story about how Tom lost his hand in the zeppelin attack on York during World War II (related later in

footnote seven), this suggests it is a collective memory uncon-
sciously triggered by the pet shop fire to which Ruby awakens. The
novel plays on the Proustian notion that memories can be triggered
by senses such as taste and smell. It also exemplifies King's contention that "collective memory is somehow available to the individual
through the memory held by places and objects" (p. 160). Specific
places in York bring to mind events in England's collective history
and objects that span the lives of different generations such as the
glass button, lucky rabbit's foot, and silver teaspoon trigger footnotes
that record Ruby's family history. Through its emphasis on memory,
the novel thus clearly suggests that Ruby's "redemption" — the title
of the final chapter — is dependent upon the redemption of both an
individual and collective past.

HISTORY: FACTS AND FICTIONS

History generally claims to give a true account of what really happened in the past and purports to offer facts about key figures and
important events. This traditional approach to history is the one
Ruby encounters at school, where she struggles to learn the battles
of the Peninsular War for her history examination. However, *Behind
the Scenes* offers an alternative view of history. As the title suggests,
Atkinson is concerned with what lies beyond authorized versions of
the past. Although there is passing reference to the Boer War and
two World Wars, the Coronation of Elizabeth II, the Festival of
Britain, the Partition of India, the assassination of John F. Kennedy,
the Russian invasion of Czechoslovakia, the 1966 World Cup final
and the Falklands War, events regarded as the defining moments of
the era remain firmly in the background. Atkinson pushes what is
central in canonical accounts of history (political leaders, monarchs,
military heroes) to the peripheries in order to foreground aspects of

history that are often overlooked. In *Behind the Scenes* the grand narrative of history is discarded as Atkinson creates a series of micro narratives about the lives of ordinary women. As Ruby traces her family history, primarily through its female line, she counters the "phallusy" of history (a male-dominated version of history that marginalizes women) and offers a woman-centerd revision of "his-story".

Behind the Scenes contests a traditional conception of history by suggesting that it is impossible to know what really happened in the past. Although the footnotes have a different tone to the main chapters and appear to be narrated by an omniscient third person narrator, they are actually narrated by Ruby: " . . .and this is the really interesting bit of my great-grandmother's story . . ." (p. 33). The realization that Ruby, an unreliable narrator, is relating the stories in the footnotes calls their accuracy into question and provides a reminder that there is no direct access to the past. Because the past is mediated, it is subject to interpretation. By using Ruby to relate both her life history and the historical flashbacks Atkinson also indicates that history is subject to the same processes as memory. The "scenes" of the novel's title point to the partial nature of history and suggest that, like Ruby's memory, history contains gaps and never tells the whole story. Symbolizing the way in which official versions of history leave out certain aspects of the past, Ruby's history teacher overlooks large sections of the syllabus: "Only when we were sitting our exam did we discover that there had been terrible battles and bloody revolutions of which we knew nothing" (p. 355). Because neither Frank, Jack nor Albert can face speaking or writing about the horror of the war, their experience goes unrecorded. Lawrence's death underlines the impossibility of establishing an accurate account of the past. As the sole witness to his mother's departure, Lawrence is the only person who knows that Alice did not die in childbirth, and history is distorted when this knowledge dies with him. Ruby is thus informed that Alice dies giving birth to Nell.

The novel encourages a skeptical view of facts, the instability of which make it impossible to verify historical truth. Fabrication is accepted as fact when Frederick tells his children that Alice has died rather than departed, and when Gillian informs her family that Ruby is responsible for Pearl's death. George's Edward VIII Coronation jug, "an item commemorating an event that never took place" (p. 82), illustrates that even official historical records can be inaccurate. Empirical evidence is equally misleading. Ruby wrongly assumes that the woman in the Lowther Street family photograph is her grandmother when it is actually Rachel, her great-grandfather's second wife. In footnote three, Bunty is misled in her belief that Edmund is not in York long enough to enjoy a drink in Betty's bar and, contrary to what the barber tells her, Mrs. Carter and Mr. Simon *are* in the bombed flat above the shop. The issue of Edmund's paternity exemplifies how easy it is to misinterpret empirical evidence. Throughout the novel various characters (and the reader) are led to believe that, because of their shared blond hair and blue eyes, Albert is Edmund's father. However, in footnote ten Lillian finally reveals that paternity belongs to Jack. Like the photograph that hides Alice's advanced state of pregnancy, this disclosure illustrates that appearances can be deceptive.

The novel further challenges the authority of facts by eroding a firm boundary between fact and fiction. Ruby's reference to real historical figures who have become either mythologized or fictionalized highlights how fact and fiction often merge: "Guy Fawkes was born here, Dick Turpin was hung a few streets and Robinson Crusoe, that other great hero, is also a native son of this city. Who is to say which of these is real and which a fiction?" (p. 10). Her presentation of history as a series of "stories" is suggestive of the fictional processes at work in history, and echoes Hayden White's assertion that historical narratives are "fictions of factual representation" or "verbal fictions, the contents of which are *as much invented as found* and the forms of which have more in common with their counterparts in literature than they have with those in history" (p. 82; p. 102). The World War I films that Lillian and Nell watch with Jack are certainly closer to fiction than fact and mythify the war by presenting it as, in Albert's words, "a bit of a lark" (p. 53). Images of the soldiers waving and smiling as they leave for the Front makes the Battle of the Somme look like "no more than a day's excursion" (p. 69). Human casualties are occluded and the absence of sound makes it seem like "a very peaceful battle" (p. 69). The films deny the atrocity of war and contradict Frank's experience of fear and chaos. As Jack explains to Nell, "It wasn't like that" (p. 69). Another discrepancy between public and private versions of history emerges in the story of Bunty's experience of World War II, which offers a revisionary history of the Blitz and undermines the myth of courageous city dwellers making do and pulling together, sustained by their "bulldog spirit" (p. 95):

By the beginning of 1942 Bunty was pretty much fed up with the war. She was sick of Dr. Carrot and Potato Pete and Mrs. Sew-and-Sew, and would have given anything for a big box of chocolates and a new winter coat and if she met the Squander Bug in the street she was personally prepared to take him round every shop in York. She really wasn't in the spirit of things at all. (p. 99)

Behind the Scenes challenges a traditional conception of history both at the level of theme and form. Linear historical time is ostensibly confirmed by the chronological dates of the main chapters but undercut by the footnotes, which persistently interrupt the present with the past and do not regress sequentially. Disrupted chronology disturbs a view of history predicated on the assumption that there is an unstoppable onward rush of time and irreversible movement from past to present. Atkinson also privileges circularity over linearity by giving both the main chapters and the footnotes a circular structure. The footnotes begin with Ruby comparing her picture of Alice with the "1914, Lowther Street" photograph and end with Lawrence deciding to return home in 1914, and the end of the novel echoes its opening through the repetition of Ruby's question about what is real (p. 10; p. 382). Similarly, although the novel begins with the conception of one life and ends with the extinction of another, the apparently linear movement from birth to death is undermined by Atkinson's use of repetition. As Ruby awaits birth and Bunty awaits death, both their lives are "hanging by a thread" (p. 26, p. 373).

HISTORY: PAST AND PRESENT

In *Behind the Scenes*, the past permeates the present and the present replicates the past. The shop ghosts and objects such as the pink glass button that goes rolling down the years bring the past into the present, and history repeats itself through the lives of successive women. Sophia, Alice, Nell, and Bunty all lead lives marred by misery, disappointment, and domestic drudgery. None of these women marry for love and all encounter marital strife. Alice, an impoverished widower, marries Frederick in order to give up teaching, Nell marries Frank out of desperation, her two previous fiancés having been killed in the war, and Bunty marries George when she is abandoned by her American fiancé, Buck. Thwarted in potential, trapped and unhappy, the women share a sense that they are living the wrong life. The loss of children is a recurring motif. When Alice elopes, she leaves her six children at the cottage; Nell's daughter,

Betty, moves to Canada and only returns to England once; Bunty loses three children (Pearl drowns, Gillian is hit by a car, and Patricia runs away); and Patricia gives up her illegitimate baby for adoption. Women of different generations also endure the loss of sisters who move away: Lillian, Nell's sister, moves to Canada, as does Bunty's sister Betty, and Patricia emigrates to Australia.

Parallels between past and present create a sense of historical inevitability that is endorsed by a series of echoes between the lives of different women. Nell falls in love with Jack who has "high, sharp cheekbones . . . like razor clam shells" (p. 50), and Ruby falls in love with an Italian who has cheeks "as sharp as knife blades" (p. 355). Bunty looks like Nell and Ruby looks like Alice. Sophia, Bunty, and Nell all suffer dementia. Ruby and Alice both believe in destiny, and each embrace "destiny" in the mistaken form of men (p. 32; p. 357). They both try to improve their foreign lovers' English. Sophia, Alice, Bunty, and Patricia all marry older men. Ada and Bunty share the same "artificial smile" (p. 112), which Ruby also borrows, and Ada and Patricia both hate to be touched. Patricia follows Lillian in having a child out of wedlock, and when Bunty and Babs tell Ruby not to be clever, they reiterate what Lillian says to Nell. Alice, Bunty, and Ruby have all "had enough" (p. 30, p. 229, p. 346).

However, *Behind the Scenes* questions historical inevitability by stressing chance and coincidence. Randomness and unpredictability are epitomized by the fate of George's father who survives the carnage of war to be run over by tram in 1945. The suggestion that life is devoid of order or rationale is accompanied by a parody of the logic of cause and effect, as when Ruby reveals what happens to Kathleen:

Her subsequent grudge against Janet Sheriff, our history teacher, will be greater than mine, for it is, after all, Miss Sheriff's amnesic love life which is directly responsible for our failing our History A Level and for Kathleen joining the Civil Service at clerical rather than administrative grade, which in turn will result in her bottom drawer expanding on credit. This will put pressure on the marriage and lead to Colin drinking, losing the family business, going bankrupt before he's forty and shooting the family dog. (p. 356)

Ruby's reference to genes initially seems to endorse a sense of destiny but Atkinson only invokes biological determinism in order to reject it. Ruby accounts for patterns in family history in terms of genes and believes that behavior is shaped by biology: "One of those curious genetic whispers across time dictates that in moments of stress we will all (Nell, Bunty, my sisters, me) brush our hands across our foreheads in exactly the same way that Alice has just done" (p. 31). The reference to genes implies that behavioral patterns are predestined and inescapable. Yet the "cherub gene" and the "housework gene" also call biological determinism into question. The cherub gene, held to be responsible for angelic looks, blond hair, forget-me-knot blue eyes, and premature death, is apparently passed down from Alice through Albert, Ada, and Edmund to Gillian and Sister Blake. However, two revelations towards the end of the novel demonstrate that the cherub gene is mythical. First, although Albert and Edmund die young men in World War I and World War II respectively, Ada dies of diptheria aged twelve, and Gillian dies in a road accident aged ten, the penultimate footnote reveals that, contrary to what her children believe, Alice lives to be an old lady. Second, the revelation that Jack, not Albert, is Edmund's father questions the existence of a cherub gene because Jack has dark hair. Atkinson also parodies biological essentialism when Ruby attributes her lack of enthusiasm for domestic chores to not having "inherited the housework genes from Auntie Babs and Bunty" (p. 354).

The recognition that biology is not destiny is crucial because it introduces the possibility of change. Historical progress is connoted by the increasing distance that successive women travel from home. Alice, who is worse off, gets nowhere. After leaving her children to venture to France with Monsieur Armand, she ends up in a situation strikingly similar to the one she sought to escape: "Finally she washed up in Sheffield, quite penniless, living in a terrace slum and taking in, not washing but other people's children, the irony of which was not lost in her" (p. 348). As a child, Nell refuses to follow Lillian as she escapes out of the bedroom window and down a tree to the fair, and remains locked in the Lowther Street house, where she spends most of the rest of her life. Desperate to join the Sunday School outing to the seaside, Bunty flees the house but, after missing the train, returns home, a pattern she repeats after Gillian's death. Patricia runs away from home and later settles in Sydney, and Ruby moves to Scotland. As the women of different generations become increasingly empowered and exert greater control over their lives, they gradually move further away from the position of their mothers — literally and metaphorically.

Ruby's rhetorical question, "Will I turn out like my mother?" (p. 280), prompts the reader to compare the lives of mother and daughter. In several ways, Ruby's life does indeed resemble that of Bunty. Repeating her mother's mistakes, Ruby finds herself peeling endless potatoes in a disastrously unhappy marriage. Intertextual allusions to *The Wizard of Oz* confirm the repetition of roles and identities. As Bunty wears red shoes, Ruby's "ruby-red slippers" imply that she will follow in her mother's footsteps (p. 112). However, in contrast to her foremothers, Ruby moves from being a passive victim to an active agent, a self-determined subject in charge of her own destiny. She breaks out of established patterns by leaving her feckless husband and finding fulfilment as a successful poet and translator. Some reviewers suggested that it was a mistake to extend the novel beyond Ruby's youth, and complained that the final scenes skirt over her adult life. Yet these scenes are crucial to the novel's overall design in demonstrating change and development. In contrast to the emphasis on Ruby's fraught relationship with her mother, the lack of detail about her daughters suggests a mother-daughter relationship that is unproblematic. Historical progress is also conveyed by the contrast between the shop parrot and the Shetland birds. Whereas Bunty is associated with the parrot that escapes and returns the same day she does, Ruby is associated with the host of wild birds that live free on her Scottish island:

Where I live you can find the red-throated diver and the eider duck, the curlew and the plover. There, there are puffins and the black guillemots, ravens and rock doves, nestling on the summer cliffs while above the moorland rise the merlin and the great skuas. (p. 382)

Ruby may initially follow in her mother's footsteps but she ultimately takes a different path, one that leads, as the last line of the novel indicates, to self-awareness and self-affirmation: "I am Ruby Lennox" (p. 381).

Although Megan Harlan dismisses the footnotes as "colorful snapshots" of the past that do little to illuminate the more compelling modern day narrative, the contrary is true. As Ruby discovers, the past illuminates the present: "The past is a cupboard full of light and all you have to do is find the key that opens the door" (p. 379). The novel insists the past must be remembered, suggests that it is necessary to know the past in order to understand the present, and demonstrates that those who do not learn from history are condemned to repeat it. In short, looking back enables Ruby to move forward. As she constructs her family history in the footnotes, Ruby's reclamation of the past creates new possibilities for the present and the future.

MOTHER-DAUGHTER RELATIONS

The subject of mother-daughter relations lies at the heart of *Behind the Scenes*. The novel examines a series of mother-daughter relationships within one family but focuses on the tensions and conflicts in Ruby's bitter relationship with Bunty, and explores what Adrienne Rich calls "the essential female tragedy" (p. 237): mother-daughter alienation. Ruby's narrative documents her mother's maternal deficiencies, recording what she calls Bunty's "autistic mothering" (p. 374). Bunty is irritable, impatient, and insensitive. Her failure is registered in Ruby's form of address: "Bunty's name will be 'Mummy' for a few years yet, of course, but after a while there won't be a single maternal noun (mummy, mum, mam, ma, mama, mom, marmee) that seems appropriate and I more or less give up calling her anything" (p. 9). Apparently incapable of affection, Bunty callously spurns Gillian's embrace and ignores her cuts and bruises when she falls off her tricycle in Museum Gardens. She curtly instructs Patricia that she does not like children and, during Patricia's phase of adolescent rebellion, locks her out of the house. She shows no interest in Ruby's school report and fails to notice signs of her daughter's suicidal despair. In short, Ruby presents her mother as a monster.

While the intensity of the first person narrative encourages identification with Ruby and generates sympathy for her position, it also produces a partial and intensely solipsistic point of view. For the greater part of the novel Ruby comprehends the world from a child's perspective and, like James' Maisie, her narrative demonstrates a child's limited understanding and lack of insight. Because Ruby represses her memory of Pearl's death, she does not realize that Bunty is in mourning when she returns from Dewsbury. When she does note her mother's distress, she is too preoccupied with her own pain to spare her sympathy. After Gillian's death, Ruby witnesses her mother "lying on her back on the bed emitting little yelps, her hands clawing the eiderdown," and hears her moaning "My baby, my baby's gone" (p. 189). However, she can only comment that this "wasn't very nice for me and Patricia" (p. 189). Although she recognizes that Bunty is "soaked in grief and tranquillizers" (p. 202), Ruby belittles her mother's suffering with sarcastic comments. She refers to the tranquillizers as "Bunty's little helpers" (p. 206), and describes a poignant outpouring of grief as Bunty's " 'My Gillian, my pearl' routine" (p. 207). Throughout the narrative, Ruby's mock expressions of pity give her account of her mother's woes a sardonic tone: "Our poor mother—can't bear us out of her sight, can't bear us in it" (p. 205). Only after she recovers her memory, and Dr. Herzmark suggests that Bunty does not hate her, can Ruby finally feel genuine pity for her mother: "Poor Bunty—losing two children" (p. 338).

However, the novel makes it possible to see Bunty in an entirely different light to the one in which Ruby presents her and generates sympathy for Bunty by telling her story. Bunty's story is embedded in the main chapters and manifests itself directly in the footnotes, which present Bunty as a woman in her own right rather than simply as a mother. Her story draws attention to the situation in which she functions as a mother, factors that shape her style of mothering, and her own experience of being mothered. If Bunty alienates her children and feels alienated from them, the novel suggests this is largely the result of the alienating circumstances in which she finds herself a mother.

Behind the Scenes provides some penetrating insights into the institution of mothering in 1950s Britain. Because George is absent from the birth, Bunty goes through labor without any emotional support. The doctor who oversees the delivery is rude and unsympathetic: "Get a move on, woman! An angry voice booms like a muffled fog-horn. 'I've got a bloody dinner party to go to!' " (p. 39). The midwife is equally unsupportive and abrasive: "She raps out her orders—'PUSH! PUSH NOW!' " (p. 39). The hospital's strict· feeding regime, which dictates that babies are fed at regular intervals regardless of whether or not they are hungry, reflects then prevailing opinion that warned against "spoiling" babies by feeding them on demand or picking them up when they cried (p. 42). Like her conscientious adherence to the advice offered in the "Bringing up Baby" section of her *Everything Within* book (p. 18), Bunty's expe- rience in hospital suggests that her style of mothering is shaped by dominant social ideas about motherhood. Ruby's sense of neglect is thus partly the product of "expert" pronouncements on how women should mother.

Bunty's domestic situation also explains her sense of alienation. George marries her because he thinks she will be "a big help in the shop" (p. 14). She marries him because, having been abandonned by Buck, the social pressure to marry leaves her desperate to find a husband: "She wasn't sure about this, but, with the war now draw- ing to a close, the possibilities were beginning to fade" (p. 108). Sex with George is emotionally sterile, something to be "endured" rather than enjoyed (p. 12), and the night that Ruby is conceived a drunken George presses himself on Bunty while she pretends to be asleep (p. 9). In an era before the advent of the contraceptive pill, the packet of condoms that Patricia finds in George's bedside-table indicates that Bunty does not have full control of her fertility. Bunty is thus less than thrilled to find herself facing an unplanned preg- nancy in a loveless marriage.

It is taken for granted by all the characters in the novel that Bunty has primary responsibility for childcare and domestic issues. George offers no help with the children or household chores and, even though he was once a corporal in the catering corps, never cooks. Yet in contrast to her complaints about her mother, Ruby overlooks the shortcomings of her father. Whereas Ruby accuses Bunty of willfully "abandoning" her children when she goes away for a week (p. 150), she notes George's persistent absence without judgement: "George is out, as usual" (p. 210). George regularly absconds from the shop, leaving Bunty to run the business, manage the home, and tend to the children. Therefore, although Ruby sarcastically mocks her mother's martyrdom — she describes Bunty as "doing her impression of the Martyred Wife" (p. 170), and refers to her as "Our Lady of the Kitchen" (p. 179) — there is evidence to suggest that Bunty's complaints are a legitimate and justifiable response to an oppressive situation. Ruby's bewilderment at the family's inability to cope when Bunty disappears indicates that her mother is consumed by a role for which she receives neither recognition nor thanks: "How is it that without Bunty around to remind us we can't do the simplest things like waking up, eating, remembering we're going on holiday?" (p. 151).

The novel creates further sympathy for Bunty by situating her performance as a mother in a historical continuum. In *Mothers and Daughters* (1992), Vivien Nice argues that a woman's relationship with her daughter is often shaped by her relationship with her mother. *Behind the Scenes* bears this out by tracing a historical pattern of women who feel insufficiently nurtured. Alice is orphaned when Sophia commits suicide, Nell is abandoned shortly after she is born when Alice elopes, and Bunty's experience of being mothered is as impoverished as that of Ruby. When Bunty misses the train for the Sunday School outing, she wets herself in distress, and returns home "looking forward to sobbing her misery into a familiar pair of arms" (p. 196). However, her anguish goes unsoothed and Bunty is left uncomforted by a mother driven to distraction by the strains of domesticity. As she grows up, Nell offers Bunty neither encouragement nor affirmation: "Nell wasn't one for compliments, she didn't like people getting above themselves"

(p. 94). Consequently, Bunty's accomplishments are "totally over-looked at home" (p. 94). Their relationship does not improve with age. When Bunty takes Gillian to visit her grandmother, Nell is equally cold: "Bunty's presence is getting on Nell's nerves and she shifts restlessly in the depths of her armchair wondering when we're going to go so she can listen to the wireless in peace" (p. 23). The distress of unmet needs causes profound emotional and psychological damage, leaving Ruby's foremothers with a lifelong yearning for mother-love. On honeymoon in the Lake District, "Nell made a horrible choking noise and wailed, 'I want my mother!'" (p. 169), and a senile Bunty asks Ruby, "You haven't seen my mother have you? I can't find her anywhere" (p. 368). A legacy of pain and privation means that successive generations of women are expected to give what they have never received: maternal love. The sugges-tion that the inability to express love is tied to the experience of feeling unloved is endorsed by the effect of Bunty's affair with Clive Roper. Once Bunty receives affection, she learns how to give it and Ruby's relationship with her mother suddenly improves:

I don't know why—probably because of her new-found skittishness in love— but these are some of the most pleasant times that Bunty and I have ever spent together. In between acquiring bits of uniform we rest up in cafes with our big paper bags. Bunty kicks off her shoes under the table in Betty's and devours a huge strawberry and meringue basket and looks almost happy. (p. 239)

Despite her shortcomings, the novel suggests that Bunty genuinely cares about her children. According to Giovanni Boccaccio's *Fa-mous Women* (1361–2)—a revision of Petrach's *Lives of Famous Men*—Bunty's namesake, Berenice, Queen of Cappadocia, loved her children fiercely. The fact that she names her twin daughters after precious stones suggests that she holds them dear, and Bunty stresses maternal love in the note she leaves George when she goes away: "you know how much I love the children" (p. 150). After Gillian's death she is plagued with anxiety about anything that could threaten the children's welfare: "we are continually assured of her maternal care for us by the stream of warnings that issue from her mouth—*Be careful with the knife! You'll poke your eye out with that pencil! Hold onto the bannister! Watch that umbrella!*" (p. 205). Bunty also expresses relief when Ruby escapes from the pet shop fire: "to my surprise she says nothing at all and pulls me towards her, wrapping me in the shelter of her dressing-gowned arms" (p. 215).

There is also evidence to suggest that Bunty is not such an appalling parent. Her comparison to Hawthorne's Hestor Prynne in *The Scarlet Letter* (1850), a woman initially regarded as a bad mother (to her daughter Pearl) but who comes to be revered as a model of goodness, implies that Ruby's mother may be misjudged. Although Ruby accuses her mother of "neglect" (p. 153), Bunty notices her knee injury and looks in on her while she is sleeping, "to check if I'm still breathing, I suppose" (p. 328). In prompting readers to ponder Ruby's question, "Is this a good mother?" (p. 20), rather than simply allowing us to revile Bunty as a bad mother, the novel implicitly reiterates Margaret Atwood's plea that women be allowed imperfections without being pronounced 'monsters, slurs, or bad examples' (p. 227). However, to resist Ruby's vilification of her mother is not to deny her experience or the pain she feels. As Hilary Mantel observes in her essay in the *London Review of Books*, Atkinson has the ability to represent opposing realities. The two competing and incompatible realities of mother and daughter create an aporia within which binary oppositions are suspended. Ultimately, *Behind the Scenes* neither condemns nor condones Bunty's performance as a parent but defies the simplistic categories of good and bad mothers.

THE MYTH OF THE PERFECT MOTHER

Ruby's dissatisfaction with Bunty stems largely from the myth of the perfect mother. She cherishes a romanticized image of an ideal mother:

I do not believe that Bunty is my real mother. My real mother is roaming in a parallel universe somewhere, ladling out mother's milk the colour of Devon cream. She's padding the hospital corridors searching for me, her fierce, hot lion-breath steaming up the cold windows. My real mother is Queen of the Night, a huge, galactic figure, treading the Milky Way in search of her lost infant. (pp. 42–3)

Ruby's ideal mother is clearly a fiction, her image shaped by fairy tales such as *Snow White*. Ruby avers that her "real" mother is "the one who dropped ruby-red blood onto a snow-white handkerchief and wished for a little girl with hair the colour of a shiny jet-black raven's wing" (p. 43). In *From the Beast to the Blonde* (1994), Marina Warner points out that many fairy tales contain "patriarchal plots" which focus on hatred between women, and notes that hostility towards the figure of the mother has become sharper in modern interpretations of classical tales (p. xxiv). Although fairy tales have no eternal or essential values, reflecting the binary oppositions that structure patriarchy, mass marketed fairy tales of the twentieth century typically divide women into two groups: good and bad. This is epitomized by *The Wizard of Oz*, which features the "Wicked Witch of the West" and Glinda, the "Good Witch of the North." As *The Wizard of Oz* demonstrates, "good" women are idealized and "bad" women are demonized. Because Bunty is human, she inevitably falls short of Ruby's ideal, and is consequently cast in the role of wicked step-mother. In *Women's Work* (1974), Ann Oakley observes that few mothers are able to provide the continual love that the myth of motherhood sets up as an ideal. The impossibility of ever being a good enough mother is demonstrated by Ruby's announcement that she does not like Bunty, which she makes while still in the womb, and her petty dissatisfaction with Bunty's name: " 'Bunty' doesn't seem like a very grown-up name to me—would I be better off with a mother with a different name?" (p. 9). The myth of the perfect mother results in Ruby's disappointment and Bunty's denigration. As Nice comments: "The idealisation of mothering sets the scene for the demonisation of the mother" (p. 135). Tragically, because Ruby is unable to see past the myth, she never really knows her mother. The night that Bunty lies dying in hospital, Ruby realizes that the woman before her is a near stranger: "I don't think I have ever looked at my mother so much as I have looked at her this night and now that I come to study her I feel as if I have no idea who she is" (p. 373).

While Ruby internalizes the myth of the perfect mother, the novel's unsentimental representation of motherhood encourages the reader to see beyond it. By exposing the chasm between myth and reality, Bunty's experience subverts several of the most enduring myths of motherhood. First, her animosity to motherhood subverts the myth of maternal instinct, which presupposes women have an innate desire to bear and care for children. As a young girl, Bunty finds baby Spencer so "disgusting" that she vows she "would *never, ever* have babies" (p. 100). When Ruby is born, she expresses revulsion and rejects her baby: "Looks like a piece of meat. Take it away" (p. 40). Statistics quoted by Oakley illustrating that a significant number of women have difficulty loving their children suggest that while Bunty's feelings of hostility and resentment may be culturally taboo, they are not uncommon.

The surrogate mothers that pervade the text also demonstrate that motherhood is not merely a matter of biology. Bunty's boss at

Modelia Fashions, Mrs. Carter, is a "real mother-hen to Bunty" (p. 93), Auntie Doreen "makes a splendid Marmee" in the Whitby performance of *Little Women* (p. 160), Dr. Herzmark tenderly rocks Ruby "like a baby" (p. 337), Mrs. von Liebnitz (Aileen McDonald) shares a blissful afternoon cooking and chatting with Ruby by the kitchen fire, and even Marjorie Morrison, who looks like "a near-relation of Mrs. Danvers," the cold and calculating housekeeper in Daphne Du Maurier's *Rebecca* (p. 353), offers Ruby comfort when she breaks down in tears in The Royal Highland Hotel. Whereas Bunty is associated with unpalatable food such as lumpy porridge, tough pork, and canned peaches with sour cream, the nurture offered by surrogate mothers is signified by satisfying and delicious treats. Doreen lets the children eat shop cakes and fish and chips, Ruby shares floury potato-scones with Mrs. von Liebniz and Dr Herzmark gives her sweets.

Second, Bunty's experience demythifies the joy of motherhood by exposing the suffering that myths make invisible. When Bunty discovers that she is pregnant, she is overwhelmed with horror rather than joy: "She sits abruptly down on the toilet and mouths a silent Munch-like scream — it can't be" (p. 26). Although Ruby complains that "Nine months of being imprisoned inside her hasn't been the most delightful of experiences" (p. 39), the pregnancy is far from delightful for Bunty either, who suffers sleepless nights and daily bouts of morning sickness. There is little evidence to suggest that Bunty's children are a source of joy either. Precocious, "cross-patch" Gillian is "born angry" (p. 40), and continues to be whiny and "demanding" (p. 13). Patricia is either "vicious" or moody, cold, and uncommunicative (p. 146). She refuses to speak when Bunty asks about her day at school, cannot stand physical contact, and is withdrawn: "even at seven, her lust for privacy is monumental and off-putting" (p. 89). Although Bunty receives little affection from her children, the myth that women possess an infinite capacity for unconditional love means that she is still expected to love them.

A third myth the novel undercuts is the myth that "motherhood represents the greatest achievement of a woman's life: the sole true means of self-realization" (Oakley, p. 186). Bunty's disgruntlement indicates that she is far from satisfied being solely a wife and mother. Moreover, her experience suggests that rather than offering a means of self-realization, motherhood demands self-denial. Bunty's quest for self-discovery conflicts with a model of motherhood that requires service, sacrifice, and selflessness. As she moves into adulthood during World War II, Bunty tries out a series of different identities in the search for selfhood: Deanna Durbin (p. 94), Scarlett O' Hara (p. 97), and Greer Garson in *Mrs. Miniver* (p. 102). However, as her family grows, her dreams diminish, and Bunty is tragically forced to forgo a self she has not yet fully realized. The erosion of self is symbolized by the abbreviation of her name from Berenice to Bunty, which George truncates to "Bunt" (p. 15).

MY MOTHER / MY SELF: THE MOTHER-DAUGHTER BOND

Nice argues that the myth of the perfect mother works to support male-dominated society by dividing mothers and daughters against each other and denying women a potentially empowering bond. In *Behind the Scenes*, annulment of the mother-daughter bond is epitomized by Ruby's persistent denial of Bunty. She suspects that she is a changeling and anticipates a death-bed confession from Bunty confirming that she is not her real mother. Nevertheless, the novel suggests that a mother-daughter bond persists despite Ruby's refusal to acknowledge it. The metaphor of the umbilical cord that Ruby uses to emphasize distance simultaneously indicates connection:

"It's a strange rule of life that no matter how quickly I walk I can never catch up with Bunty—slow or fast, she's always at least three feet in front of me as if there's an invisible umbilical cord between us that can stretch but never contract" (p. 203). This bond takes Ruby by surprise when she gets married: "Bunty refuses to speak to me for over a year and I am horrified to find that I miss her" (p. 358).

Although Ruby repeatedly denies her mother, Bunty's death brings a sense of acceptance: "I had thought that when she died it would be like having a weight removed and I would rise up and be free of her, but now I realize that she'll always be here, inside me" (p. 376). Alienation dissolves into resignation, and while Bunty may not be absolved, the mother-daughter bond is redeemed. The novel uses a series of literal and figurative mirrors to reflect Ruby's changing attitude to her mother. At Sandra and Ted's wedding, she sees Bunty's image reflected to infinity in bathroom mirrors, and feels disturbed by a "vision of a mother who seems to go on for ever" (p. 292). However, after her mother's death, Ruby recognizes that Bunty lives on through her: "I suppose when I'm least expecting it I'll look in the mirror and see her expression or open my mouth and speak her words" (p. 376). Ruby's recognition of the way in which mother and daughter mirror each other is prefigured by allusions to *The Wizard of Oz*. Ruby may resemble Dorothy most closely in her search for home, but mother and daughter both function as Dorothy figures. Bunty not only wears red shoes, but almost moved to Kansas, and thinks of Edmund as "a great golden-velvet lion" (p. 106). Echoing psychoanalytic interpretations of *The Wizard of Oz* that read the tornado as a manifestation of Dorothy's rage and frustration, Bunty "feels as if the top of her head's going to come off and a cyclone is going to rip out of her brain and tear up everything around her" (p. 24). Affinities between mother and daughter are reinforced by color symbolism. Bunty wears ruby-red lipstsick as well as red shoes, sees herself as Scarlett O'Hara, and takes the part of Miss Scarlet in Cluedo. As Ruby's allusion to Hawthorne's *The Scarlet Letter* implies, Bunty's affair with Clive Roper also casts her in the role of a "scarlet woman" (p. 250): "the offending couple are vertical and looking modestly decent, but I think we can all see the blazing scarlet letter 'A' branded across Bunty's beige turtle-neck sweater" (p. 264). Because Bunty's death enables Ruby to acknowledge these affinities, her acceptance of her mother signals self-acceptance. The "redemption" of the last chapter thus lies at least partly in Ruby's realization that she no longer has to deny her mother to affirm herself (p. 366).

ENGLAND AND ENGLISHNESS

During the 1990s several events bought the issue of national identity to prominence in Britain. The move towards European federalism and campaigns for Scottish and Welsh independence bought questions of nation sharply into focus and the nation itself into question. Such events prompted reflection on what it means to be British. When New Labour came to power in 1997, Tony Blair sought to move away from Britain's imperial past and modernize its image by reinventing the country as "Cool Britannia". This re-evaluation of Britishness entailed a pointed re-evaluation of Englishness. No longer taken as the self-evident norm against which other identities were defined, in the late twentieth century Englishness came under a newly self-conscious critical scrutiny.

Behind the Scenes explores what it means to be English by examining established definitions of national identity. It contests dominant ideas and images of England and debunks deeply entrenched myths of Englishness. The novel rejects a literary inheritence that idealizes England as a "green and pleasant land" or a "land of hope and glory" and, in contrast to literary predecessors such as Rupert Brook and Evelyn Waugh, Atkinson refuses to represent England with a sense of piety, whimsy, or sentimentality. Indeed, the novel exhibits disdain for the dominant ideology of Englishness. Englishness, defined against and dependent upon the construction of "otherness", is exposed as a politically motivated concept that works to establish the hegemony of England by marginalizing other national identities. Atkinson exposes cracks and contradictions in the ideology of Englishness and challenges the status quo by re-presenting the nation in a way that gives prominence to voices that are usually denied, and aspects of national identity frequently repressed, in the dominant discourse of nation.

Bunty personifies the dominant version of English national identity prevalent in the period. Described as "the flower of English womanhood" (p. 19), she is patriotic, insular, xenophobic, and intensely class conscious. When she hears that war has been declared between Britain and Germany, Bunty stands to exclaim "Rule Britannia!" (p. 95), and when she meets her Canadian cousin Edmund for the first time, she greets him reticently, "with a good deal of national reserve" (p. 104). Furthermore, she is suspicious of, and hostile to, the unfamiliar: "Bunty does not like foreign food. She has not actually tasted any foreign food but nonetheless she knows she doesn't like it" (p. 236). As these examples illustrate, a strong sense of national identity requires the disavowal of difference. The local concentration camp that houses "aliens", the racial harassment that Bunty's Hunagarian boss, Mr. Simon, suffers during the war, and Clifford's enthusiasm for the "the subject of repatriating the 'blacks' " are all the product of categories of inclusion and exclusion that underpin national identity (p. 377). Ruby's distance from the model of womanhood and nationhood represented by her mother is measured by her different attitude to "otherness": whereas Bunty makes "Dago Cakes" (p. 78), Ruby marries an Italian.

While the novel recalls Napoleon's description of the English as "a nation of shopkeepers," Bunty's role as a representative of Englishness is underlined by two specific figures with whom she identifies. In her fantasy life, Bunty "bears a passing resemblance to Celia Johnson" (p. 14), the actress who played the heroine in David Lean's classic film *Brief Encounter* (1945), whose brisk, cheerful and sensible "niceness" made her, according to Alison Light in her book *Forever England* (1991), an "icon of Englishness" (p. 208). During a moment of patriotic zeal as her "heart swelled with pride and wartime spirit" (p. 102), Bunty also sees herself as Greer Garson in the MGM film *Mrs. Miniver* (1942), a figure who, Light suggests, became "the epitome of the wartime spirit of England" (p. 113). Although women are employed as icons and symbols of nationhood (Britannia, for example), men traditionally represent the nation. The politicians and public figures recorded by historians of the period are almost exclusively male (Winston Churchill, Aneurin Bevin, William Beverage) and the literary canon is dominated by the work of male authors (W.H. Auden, T.S. Eliot, George Orwell). Given this, Bunty's role as a representative of Englishness, even a conservative version of Englishness, is radical and reflects Light's assertion that, in a historical moment in which the domestic sphere and private life represented national character, women came "to speak for the nation" (p. 146). As she argues: "Statistically and symbolically, women became the nation between the wars" (p. 210). In making Bunty the novel's major representative of Englishness, Atkinson thus participates in the revision of male-dominated versions of history.

Although Bunty identifies with the characters played by Celia Johnson and Greer Garson, she is not at all like them. She does not share Laura Jesson's niceness and crisp commonsense nor Mrs. Miniver's cheerfulness and breezy optimism. Unlike the stoical heroine in *Brief Encounter*, Bunty is vociferous about her woes and does not deny her sexual desire but enters into an extra-marital affair with the nextdoor neighbor, Mr. Roper. Unlike Mrs. Miniver, she is not devoted to the domestic and a charmed life eludes her. The contrast between Bunty and her screen idols suggests that they represent a fictional ideal of English womanhood, and exposes a schism between imaginary and real forms of national identity. In this way, the novel suggests that national identity is fundamentally an idea or state of mind, and that nation is, as Benedict Anderson proposes, an imagined community. Patricia's *Daily Graphic Coronation Book*, which contains a chapter outlining "the duties of all the boys and girls who 'will be the grown-up citizens of a new Elizabethan age' " also suggests that Englishness is a fiction and endorses Homi Bhabha's contention that nation is constructed through narration. According to Bhabha, the nation is a discursive construct or narrative strategy, and nationality a matter of 'textual affiliation' (p. 140). Construction is emphasized in Ruby's description of York, after the city has been transformed by a heritage industry that promotes a mythic image of England: "It seems like a fake city, a progression of flats and sets and white cardboard battlements and medieval half-timbered house kits that have been cut and glued together" (p. 377).

Behind the Scenes not only exposes Englishness as a construct, but also calls the every concept of Englishness into question. The various references to Vikings and Romans that scatter the novel serve as a reminder that the English descend from a host of different peoples and that Englishness has been shaped by numerous influences: "Everyone has left something here — the unnamed tribes, the Celts, the Romans, the Vikings, the Saxons, the Normans and all those who came after, they have all left their lost property" (p. 379). As Jeremy Paxman writes in *The English* (1998): "the first thing you discover about the English is that they are not English — in the sense of coming from England — at all. They had arrived from

Jutland, Anglen and Lower Saxony. The 'English race', if such a thing exists, is German" (p. 54). Like King George I (German), and the current Duke of Edinburgh (Greek), many of the nation's heads of state have been foreign. Even Winston Churchill, often regarded as a personification of the "British Bulldog," was half American, and St. George, the patron saint of England, currently serves Portugal as well as having acted variously as guardian of Malta, Sicily, Genoa, Venice, Aragon, Valencia, and Barcelona. Nowhere is the hybridity of the English clearer than in the English language, which is shaped by multiple influences. Exemplifying this hybridity, the house ghosts speak "Latin, Saxon, Norman-French" (p. 378). The realization that Englishness is not innate or discrete, that in Paxman's words, "the English are a mongrel race" (p. 59), is significant because it undermines racist objections to multiculturalism such as those uttered by John Townend, the Conservative MP for Yorkshire East who complained, in March 2001, that Britain's "homogenous Anglo-Saxon society has been seriously undermined by massive immigration."

In its celebration of a country that is "still the leader of western civilisation" (p. 90), Patricia's coronation book endorses the myth of national superiority. The myth of English pre-eminence, based on assertions of imperial greatness was revived by Margaret Thatcher's national triumphalism and her attempt to put the "great" back into "Great Britain" during the 1980s. However, the novel undermines this myth through references to Vikings and Romans, which provide a valuable reminder that Britain, a major colonizing power in the nineteenth century, was itself once colonized. Atkinson thus uses history to illustrate that positions of power are not fixed and stable, and to demonstrate that there is nothing inherently superior about the English. An English sense of superiority is also undercut by the novel's portrayal of non-English characters, who are consistently presented in a more flattering light than their English counterparts.

In particular, non-English women are notably more maternal than Bunty: Auntie Doreen is Irish, Dr. Herzmark is German, and Mrs. von Liebniz (or Aileen McDonald) and Marjorie Morrison are both Scottish. When Ruby asserts her own Scottishness, she not only rejects England but resists a grand narrative of nationhood in which Scotland is often subsumed by or seen as synonymous with England. In other words, Ruby's Scottishness resists English hegemony.

Behind the Scenes also debunks the myth of national unity. John McLeod observes that history reaffirms national identity by constructing a common past that engenders a sense of collectivity and belonging. As he states: "nations are often underwritten by the positing of a common historical archive that enshrines the common past of a collective people" (p. 70). Like the nation itself, Ruby's family gathers to watch the coronation on television. Superficially, the scene suggests a nation united by a shared history, but the domestic disharmony that erupts Above the Shop points to the illusory and mythic nature of national unity: Bunty and Babs are engaged in a baking competition; the group are divided by their argument about the chronological order of monarchs; Bunty wishes that George's lower class relatives were not there, and Gillian attacks Ruby for riding her Mobo horse. Like the fight that breaks out at Sandra and Ted's wedding as the rest of the country celebrates England's World Cup victory, the discord of the coronation scene exposes the U.K. as a fundamentally disunited kingdom.

Another key myth that Atkinson debunks is the myth of rural England. The Tory Prime Minister John Major sought to endorse the myth that England is "a green and pleasant land" in the 1990s when he claimed that, "Fifty years from now, Britain will still be the country of long shadows on county grounds, warm beer, invincible green suburbs, dog lovers and pools fillers and—as George Orwell said—'old maids' cycling to holy communion through the morning mist" (Paxman, p. 142). As Major's comments illustrate, even though England has been an overwhelmingly urban society since the mid-twentieth century, rural England still represents the nation's ideal self-image. The novel exposes this image as inaccurate and unrepresentative. Alice's experience of country living subverts the idea of a rural idyll: "The whole effect is as if someone had taken an idyllic rural scene and set it slightly off-key—the sun is too hot, the light too bright, the fields too arid, the animals too thin" (p. 30). Ruby's comment about the "Ye olde England" calender makes it clear that the dominant myth of England as a pastoral idyll does not reflect the reality of the majority: "This ye olde England is not a country we're very well acquainted with in our family—page after page, month after month, of thatched cottages, distant spires, haywains and milkmaids" (p. 222). When Ruby stubs out Patricia's cigarette on the calender, she dismisses this romantic myth of rural England.

If an idealized, mythic England is rural rather than urban it is also synonymous with the south. By giving her novel a "provincial" northern setting Atkinson resists London's status as the metropolitan center and disrupts conventional definitions of centre and periphery (p. 352). The novel also challenges stereotypes of the North and, particularly, Yorkshire. *Behind the Scenes* features no whippets, noble mills, or romantic moors and Ruby's York is not the quaint picture-postcard city of a tourist industry that seeks to turn England into a living museum. Ruby does however witness the pernicious effects of the commercialization of culture and a tourist industry that only preserves parts of the past from which it can profit when she returns to York towards the end of the novel. Above the Shop has been converted into an expensive tourist "tea-room" and York feels like "one big, incredibly expensive souvenir shop" (p. 378).

In deconstructing myths of Englishness, the novel highlights the intersection of ideologies of gender and nation. The World Cup final epitomizes women's exclusion from prevailing (patriarchal) versions of Englishness. Although the day of the World Cup final is regarded as a "day of national importance" (p. 287), only the men at Sandra and Ted's wedding reception are interested in watching the game on television and the women do not rejoice at England's victory. The women's general dissatisfaction with England is expressed in their departure. All of the characters who find happiness do so by making their home elsewhere and, as successive female characters emigrate, the novel suggests that England offers women as little hope as it does glory. Although *Behind the Scenes* focuses on women of a different social class to those discussed by Virginia Woolf in *Three Guineas* (1938), it nevertheless echoes her assertion that England's daughters "have very little to thank England for" (p. 233).

HOME

Allusions to *The Wizard of Oz* serve several functions in the text but their primary significance lies in foregrounding the theme of home. References to the 1939 MGM film version of L. Frank Baum's *The Wizard of Oz* include the Emerald City, the yellow brick road, the iconic ruby slippers, and the film's songs ("We're Off to See the Wizard" and "Somewhere Over the Rainbow"). The film's plot traces Dorothy's attempt to find her way back to her family in Kansas after she is transported to the fantastical land of Oz by a tornado, and ends with her famously cliched and saccharine homage to home. Ruby shares Dorothy's conviction that "there's no place like home" and, like Dorothy, initially associates home with family. Specifically, Ruby associates home with her mother and the pleasure of being in the womb, her first home: "I tap my tiny naked heels together three times and think, there's no place like home" (p. 25). Exiled to Auntie Babs' house in Dewsbury, Ruby uses "Kansas" as a synonym for "home" — "I don't think this is Kansas, Teddy" (p. 111) — and soon feels desperate to return to York: "I want to go home!" (p. 116).

However, *Behind the Scenes* both invokes and revises *The Wizard of Oz*. Like Salman Rushdie, Atkinson challenges a conventional definition of home as the place of origin. In his critical study, *The Wizard of Oz* (1992), Rushdie proposes that the film's images undercut its rhetoric, and argues that it is impossible to believe that Dorothy prefers Kansas to Oz, when Kansas is dull and grey and Oz is a colorful and exciting land of adventure. Rushdie therefore asserts that *The Wizard of Oz* is less a celebration of home than "a celebration of Escape, a grand paean to the Uprooted Self, a hymn — *the* hymn — to Elsewhere" (p. 23). He concludes:

the truth is that once we have left our childhood places and started to make up our lives, armed only with what we have and are, we understand that the real secret of the ruby slippers is not that 'there's no place like home', but rather that there is no longer any such place *as* home: except, of course, for the home we make, or the homes that are made for us, in Oz: which is anywhere, and everywhere, except the place from which we began. (p. 57)

Ruby's experience endorses Rushdie's thesis. As she feels increasingly rejected by Bunty, Ruby feels less and less at home in her family environment, the unhomeliness of which is signified by the house ghosts. Freud, who cites ghosts as an example of the uncanny, points out that the German "unheimlich" means both "uncanny" and "unhomely" (v. 17, p. 219). The unhomely character of life in the Lennox household exposes the hollowness of conventional assumptions about home: "Home! Sweet Home. There is no place like it. Keep its fires burning. It's where the heart is" (p. 124). When Christine Roper plays "Home Sweet Home" on the piano on holiday in Scotland, Ruby remarks that it is "a song whose popularity Patricia and I have never understood" (p. 259), and the unhomeliness of home leads both sisters to leave York, and even England, for elsewhere. Within the intertextual framework of *The Wizard of Oz*, the unhomeliness of England is signified by its affinities to Oz. The Skylon tower makes London look "like a city of the future, a science-fiction Oz" (p. 20), and its Exhibition Halls and Dome of Discovery make it "the shimmering emerald city of tomorrow" (p. 26). However, the novel ruptures *The Wizard of Oz*'s binary opposition between home (Kansas) and not-home (Oz), because Patricia eventually makes her home in Australia, the country colloquially known as "Oz". Ruby settles in Scotland but, as a poet and translator, finds her ultimate home in language. As the Polish émigré and Nobel Prize winning poet Czeslaw Milosz comments, "language is the only homeland" (Marshall, p. 7).

Returning to a consideration of the novel as a narrative of development, it is worth noting that *Behind the Scenes* significantly revises the tradition of the "bildungsroman" on which it draws. Ruby's closing remarks about writing suggest that language not only furnishes her with a home but also an identity. Ruby uses language to find meaning in her life: "In the end, it is my belief, words are the only things that can construct a world that makes sense" (p. 382). In contrast to the traditional "bildungsroman", *Behind the Scenes* suggests that identity is constructed rather than discovered, and constituted through narrative. Ruby constructs her self as she constructs her story. Furthermore, whereas the "bildungsroman" tends to be based on a humanist conception of identity as singular and static, Ruby's self is plural, provisional, and in process. Atkinson departs from a bourgeois tradition of individualism by emphasizing the intersection of different women's stories, and the novel resists closure through the suggestion that Ruby's sense of self will be endlessly (re)negotiated through a series of ongoing "stories" about her whole family: "any day now I intend to begin work on a grand project—a cycle of poems based on the family tree" (p. 382). The novel also extends Ruby's quest for understanding out from her individual and familial world to the social world she inhabits, interweaving personal and political issues through the deconstruction of myth. As a narrative of female development, *Behind the Scenes* therefore constitutes a politically-engaged, pro-feminist, postmodern reconstruction of the "bildungsroman."

3

The Novel's Reception

Behind the Scenes was greeted with lavish praise upon publication in Britain and the States and won rave reviews in many other countries, notably France. Acclaimed by critics and readers alike, its popularity was as much the result of personal recommendation as professional review, and it was already ranked number five in a British bestseller list when it won the Whitbread Prize. In Britain, Mary Louden eulogized the novel in *The Times*. Declaring it "an astounding book," she wrote:

Behind the Scenes at the Museum is without doubt one of the finest novels I have read for years. If Atkinson's publishers do not enter it for every prize going, then I will personally storm their offices to remind them of their duty to one of the most fluent and inventive new writers around.

Natasha Walter described Atkinson as a writer who started her career "hearing her own music and singing her own songs." Hilary Mantel also praised the book's originality: "it makes most English fiction look chlorotic, greensick, an exhausted swooner fanning herself in the twilight of tradition." This enthusiasm was shared by many others. Rejecting Lola Young's suggestion that writing by British women is "piddling" and "parochial" in comparison to that of American counterparts (a view she voiced as Chair of Judges for the 1999 Orange Prize), Maggie Traugott wrote in the *Independent on Sunday*: "Anyone who thinks that all the sassy new writing by women is from North America should check out this gem from Yorkshire." Across the Atlantic, Georgia Jones-Davis' review in *The LA Times* applauded what she called a "marvelous story . . . a powerhouse of storytelling, a treasure chest," and in *The New York Times Book Review* Ben Macintyre praised the book's freshness and vitality, declaring Atkinson's debut a "remarkable first novel . . . one of the funniest works of fiction to come out of Britain in years." Readers loved the novel's humor, passion and freshness. Reviewers found themselves captivated by Ruby's voice and seduced by Atkinson's prose. In the *Sunday Express*, Sally Staples described the novel as "beautifully written," and Louden wrote: "Atkinson has 'a remarkable way with words' . . . her prose is really poetry in disguise." Overall, the novel was deemed immensely readable and infinitely re-readable.

Despite this warm reception, when Atkinson won the 1995 Whitbread Book of the Year award the success of *Behind the Scenes* was greeted with surprise, even hostility, in certain enclaves of the British press. The judges' preference for *Behind the Scenes* over the two favorites, Salman Rushdie's *The Moor's Last Sigh* and Roy Jenkins's biography of Gladstone, caused a scandal. Atkinson was considered a "startling choice," and dubbed "the surprise star of 1995." Controversy centerd on the fact that a former Booker Prize winner (Rushdie) and an Oxford don (Jenkins) could be beaten by a first time female novelist and outsider to the Establishment or, in A.N. Wilson's words, an "unheard-of mental-health nurse from Yorkshire." Before Atkinson, only two other overall winners had ever come from the First Novel category and only one other woman had ever won the Book of the Year since its inception in 1985. Headlines such as "Rushdie takes 2nd prize" in *The New York Times* and "Rushdie makes it a losing double" in *The Guardian* implied that the Whitbread was Rushdie's by right and slighted Atkinson's achievement by suggesting that she had not so much won the prize as Rushdie lost it. Like the headline in *The New York Times*, several reports implied that Rushdie deserved to win especially because he had missed out on another major award the previous year when Pat Barker's *The Ghost Road* (1995) won the Booker. To lose one prize to a woman was considered unfortunate, to lose two was criminal.

A period of mean-spirited and misogynistic sniping ensued. In a *Daily Mail* article entitled "All chattering—but no class" Andrew Neil dismissed Atkinson's novel as "dull and uninspired" on the basis of a brief extract read out at the Whitbread dinner. His comment that "Even the children's book on the short list was more interesting" was obviously meant as a smear, although it is not clear who is most maligned by his remark, Atkinson or Michael Morpurgo (winner of the Best Children's Book category). Neil expressed disbelief at the judges' decision, a result he took as "simply further confirmation of why the chattering classes deserve to be held in such contempt." Sir Julian Critchley, one of the Whitbread judges, also felt aggrieved by what he considered to be the injustice of the panel's decision. *The Independent*'s "Diary" revealed that before the announcement of the prize, Critchley vigorously canvassed support for Lord Jenkins, chancellor of the University of Oxford (his alma mater), on the grounds that "a vote for Gladstone would make the claret flow in celebration among the dreaming spires," an argument that obviously left his co-judges unpursuaded as in the end Jenkins' biography received only a single vote (Critchley's own). Disgruntled by the notion that the masterpieces of English literature are no longer the preserve of the masters, Critchley published an article called "Why Roy Jenkins was Robbed" in the *Daily Telegraph* in

which he not only insults Atkinson but also his co-judges (as well as
Salman Rushdie, for whose novel the greatest praise he can muster
is that he managed to finish reading it). Critchley describes the
panel's decision as "astonishing," and proceeds to question the authority of a number of its female members. He notes that Jane Asher
"is in the process of writing her first novel" and "runs her own cake-
making business," adding "I last saw her making up to Lloyd Gross-
man on *Masterchef*." His terse assessment of Candia McWilliam is
that "she has written three good novels and borne three children."
Critchley's irrelevant comments about cooking and children expose
his contempt for the domestic and imply that baking and birth
somehow make women unsuitable arbiters of literary merit. He also
attributes Atkinson's success to a female conspiracy, speculating that
the "Corps of Lady Novelists" (as he refers to the women writers on
the panel) cast their votes on the basis of sisterly allegiance rather
than literary excellence. Hilary Mantel, who judged the First Novel
category of the Whitbread Prize along with Rachel Cusk and Jason
Cowley, came to Atkinson's defence. In an eloquent and lively essay
published in the *London Review of Books*, she condemns the media's ignorant and condescending treatment of Atkinson. Mantel's
essay offers an insightful analysis of the bigotry that still beleaguers
women writers, but a more pithy comment made by Cusk serves as
an apposite summary of the competition and its ensuing controversy. Reflecting on the Whitbread, Cusk opined, "it is hard to get
the boorishness of beer out of the Book of the Year."

Bigotry was also evident in the reviews and interviews that followed the Whitbread. Demonstrating that women are still subject
to a patriarchal tradition of criticism that is more concerned with
judging the woman than her work, several female journalists exhibited a fascination with Atkinson's appearance and deportment, about
which they felt permitted to pass comment in the most condescending manner. In *The Guardian*, Megan Tressider described Atkinson

as a "taut-featured, youthful 44 year old" and wrote, "She is wearing an expensive looking suit, a black velvet waistcoat, and has painted nails and sleek, bobbed hair." Noting that Atkinson laughs as she talks, Tressider patronizingly surmised that her "giggles" were "probably due to nervousness at being thrust into the news suddenly." Atkinson's hair and nails also fascinated Rosemary Goring: "she has hair the colour of pennies and painted nails that fly around as she talks." Cleave shared Tressider's interest in the clothes: "she wore an amazing purple knitted wool suit . . . Kate Atkinson looks glamorous in photographs, beautiful in an uncontrived way in everyday life." Jane Kelly, of the *Daily Mail*, was less kind, and deemed it newsworthy to report that she found Atkinson "pale, rather pimply, her hair unwashed." As Mantel observes, such remarks point to the persistence of a critical double standard: "Hundreds and thousands of words have been written about Salman Rushdie — and we know nothing of his manicure." The media representation of Atkinson provides an example how women are taught to identify against themselves by acting as agents of patriarchy. It is a tragic irony that the author of a book that explores the difficulty of female relations in a male-dominated world should receive such unjust treatment from other women.

While female journalists dissected Atkinson's appearance, male members of the press demonstrated an obsession with her brief stint as a chambermaid befitting a *Carry On* film. Mike Ellison's article in *The Guardian* opened, "A 44-year-old chambermaid won one of Britain's leading literary awards last night." In the *Daily Telegraph* Dan Conaghan began his report, "A first novel by a former chambermaid and teacher confounded all expectations to take the 1995 Whitbread Book of the Year." Reporters singled out this job for attention among several others, so that Atkinson came to be defined by a temporary job she held between school and college rather than any of the other posts she has occupied, including university tutor.

In addition, male and female journalists exhibited equal consternation at the contentment Atkinson expressed in her status as a twice-divorced single mother of two, and clearly found the notion that it is possible for a woman to live a happy and fulfilled life without a man quite a novelty.

On the whole, *Behind the Scenes* received a number of insightful and sensitive reviews before the Whitbread. In contrast, post-prize reviews, when they turned their attention to the novel, generated a furor around what was caricatured as Atkinson's "crazed feminism." Unsettled by her representation of miserable marriages and domestic drudgery, conservative reviewers branded the novel anti-family, feminist nonsense. After slating *Behind the Scenes*, Neil dubbed its author "Kate 'the family is tyranny' Atkinson." Kelly accused Atkinson of having "strikingly unfriendly attitudes towards men," and described her as the writer "who rejects marriage and the family, and believes we should live in tribes ruled by women." This gross misrepresentation of Atkinson as a man-hating separatist was the combined product of the media's penchant for sensation and a desire to discredit a subversive novel that some members of society found profoundly threatening.

While *Behind the Scenes* is unapologetically woman-centered, it is not at all unsympathetic to men, and accusations of this sort betray another critical double standard. The reception of *Behind the Scenes* exemplifies how novels that decentre men cause outcry while texts that marginalize women are accepted as central to the literary canon. There are no women in Herman Melville's *Moby Dick* (1851) and Joseph Conrad's *Heart of Darkness* (1899) features a small number of anonymous female characters. Yet, overlooking the fact that, as Monique Wittig puts it, "one out of two men is a woman" (p. 56), critics have long heralded these two texts as works of genius that explore a universal human condition. While the woman-centredness of *Behind the Scenes* challenges the "male-as norm-syndrome," it does more than simply invert a sexist literary tradition. Atkinson's male characters may be minor players but the novel's critique of male-dominated institutions includes an exploration of the ways in which patriarchy is harmful to men as well as women. Astute critics praised the novel's sensitive representation of male experience. In *The New York Times Book Review*, Ben Macintyre wrote: "Her description of Ruby's male forbears staggering blindly through the mud of the Somme ... is one of the most gripping and sincere depictions of war I have read." Geoff Barton agreed, stating in the *Times Educational Supplement* that, "The First World War Scenes are especially affecting." In considering Tressider's assertion that *Behind the Scenes* "got right up men's noses," it is also worth noting that male and female characters are presented in an equally unfavorable light. The portrait of Bunty as an inadequate mother is as (if not more) negative as the portrait of George as a philandering father, and the only character who has absolutely no redeeming features is female: Ruby's detestable sister, Gillian.

A reductive focus on Atkinson's portrayal of the family produced a distorted view of the book's scope and character. Kelly, for example, described it as "entirely domestic". Like Kelly, most reviewers missed connections between the personal and political, and overlooked themes such as national identity. Assumptions about the personal nature of women's writing also resulted in the relentless suggestion that the novel is autobiographical. Commentators were apt to express disappointment upon discovering that Kate Atkinson is not Ruby Lennox. Tressider described meeting Atkinson as like expecting Yorkshire pudding and getting sushi, and griped, "She doesn't even have a Yorkshire accent." Like most fiction, *Behind the Scenes* contains details drawn from its author's life. Atkinson was born in the same year as Ruby and lived above a medical and surgical supplies shop in York. She learned to read with the *Lady-*

bird Book of Puppies and Kittens, and had both a teddy and a mobo horse. She admits that writing *Behind the Scenes* was a way of finding a place for things in her life. However, while the emotions of the book are hers, the situations are not, and the novel is not autobiographical. Despite the assertion that Atkinson could not have written such a moving account of Bunty's mental disintegration without personal experience of a mother who suffered from Alzheimer's Disease, her mother was alive and well at the time of the novel's publication. The common belief that fiction by women is autobiographical (Jeanette Winterson encountered the same phenomenon when *Oranges Are Not the Only Fruit* won the Whitbread First Novel Award in 1985) stems from an underlying assumption that women restrict their writing to what they know. This assumption situates writing by women in the realm of experience rather than imagination and undermines their achievement as writers. By refusing to credit women with the creative power to transform life into literature, it implies that imagination is the sole preserve of men. Atkinson admits that she is perturbed when people mistake her fiction for autobiography, and is keen to differentiate the two: "I write fiction, I don't write autobiography and to me they are very different things. The first-person narrative is a very intimate thing, but you are not addressing other people as 'I' — you are inhabiting that 'I'." In an effort to confound the assumption that her work is autobiographical, she set her second novel in an imaginary location. Even though the setting of *Human Croquet* is invented, a number of readers still think it is in Yorkshire.

The novel also wrong-footed critics on the issue of class. Reviewers failed to come to a consensus about whether the Lennox family are working class or middle class, when in fact they are neither. Atkinson explains: "As someone once said, there is working class, middle class, upper class and then there are shopkeepers." Like Atkinson's own upwardly mobile parents, Bunty has bourgeois pretensions. She is the proud owner of the first television set in the family (the second in the street) and moves to a centrally heated "light-and-airy pebble-dashed semi" (p. 223). Overlooking the finer details of the novel, several reviewers resorted to easy assumptions and pre-conceived ideas that associate the North of England with working class fiction. Natasha Walter, for example, described her as "the Mike Leigh of novel-writing, with a dash more mystery and depth." The implicit equation of northern, working-class fiction with gritty realism left critics faced with burlesque either bemused or overwhelmed. Barton, for example, remarked, "I'm not sure the hyperbole has done the novel or its author many favours," and, writing in *The Christian Science Monitor*, Merle Rubin suggested the novel "may be a little too relentlessly flippant for some tastes." Ignoring Atkinson's defiance of convention, critics attempted to force the novel into standard categories. Despite featuring footnotes, ghosts and a narrator who can read as soon as she is born, Bernard Bergonzi claimed that Atkinson "shows that the traditional realistic novel, so often dismissed by literary theorists, still has plenty of life in it." Richard Hoggart recognised Atkinson's irreverence for convention but, not wishing to give her credit for the novel's innovations, patronizingly remarked: "I don't know if Kate Atkinson knew she was being wildly post-modernist" (qtd. Conaghan).

Confident of her talent, Atkinson has ignored superficial and unsympathetic critical responses, and remains true to her artistic ideals. *Behind the Scenes* weathered the storm of controversy that followed the Whitbread Prize and outshone the pettiness and prejudice that irritated its otherwise overwhelmingly enthusiastic reception. As Mantel predicted, it is a book that continues to dazzle readers and remains a rare thing in the literary world: a popular and critical success.

4

The Novel's Performance

Behind the Scenes spent more than a year in the bestseller lists and has sold over 500,000 copies in Britain. It was featured on BBC Radio 4's *A Good Read* and has been translated into more than fifteen languages. It has been adapted for radio, stage, and screen, and exists in two audio versions, one published by Harper Collins, and the other (an unabridged version lasting 12 hours and 20 minutes) by Chivers.

The novel was adapted for radio by Bryony Lavery, one of Britain's foremost playwrights, produced by Polly Thomas, and broadcast on BBC Radio 4 in August 2000. Lavery, who describes herself as "addicted to the idea of disturbing the air," was attracted to the novel's warmth and daring. She wrote the radio play while in the process of adapting *Behind the Scenes* for the stage. Her original plan was to record the stage version for radio but a disrupted schedule meant that the date of the radio play fell first. Lavery compares the novel to a crystal — "Every time I worked on it, I would find another refraction" — and although she sought to capture the novel's thematic complexity, a budget that only permitted six actors and ninety minutes for the performance forced her to compress and focus on Ruby's story.

The stage play, directed by Damien Cruden, appeared later the same year at the Theatre Royal, York. After falling in love with Atkinson's "beautiful, rich, original" writing, Lavery began the process of adaptation by seeking a shape or form in which to pour the novel into its new life on stage. While keen to be faithful to the novel, she recognized the necessity of change. The challenge Lavery faced was thus how to make alterations without colonizing the text, to innovate rather than dominate. Lavery's most significant change was the introduction of Herzmark at the beginning of the play. Using sessions with the psychiatrist as a device for entering Ruby's memory enabled her to keep a first person narrative. Ruby recalls the past while talking to Herzmark, and Herzmark guides Ruby, along with the audience, through the story. As in the novel, Ruby's story takes precedence, but Lavery resisted the temptation to focus on Ruby exclusively and felt it was important to include all the other generations, "because that is what makes the book mighty in its highly original way." One of the greatest challenges posed by the novel was its range. Some characters and scenes had to be cut — for example, the audience does not see Ruby after age sixteen — and Lavery is rather wistful about this loss: "In retrospect, it would be great fun to do a long version of *Behind the Scenes* . . . a come-for-the-day-and-bring-sandwiches version!" Nevertheless, she was happy with the play's success: "Watching the York production, it seemed to me that we achieved something quite theatrically magical. I could feel the rapt silence of the audience, the laughter, and the grief they felt at the end." Atkinson, who attended the opening night, commended the play and the performance received enthusiastic reviews. Writing in the *Daily Mail*, Michael Coveney praised the way in which Lavery "niftily filleted" the novel for the stage, noting that the characters are "all lifted perfectly onto the stage."

He concluded, "the black farce and sardonic tone of Atkinson's writing are beautifully transcribed in text and action."

As this book goes to press, Atkinson is in the process of adapting *Behind the Scenes* for BBC television. The screenplay is due to be broadcast in the form of three one-hour episodes in 2002. Atkinson agreed to turn the novel into a screenplay because she loves television. She once remarked that she could watch *Antiques Roadshow* all day and declared appearing on the lifestyle program, *This Morning*, the pinnacle of her success: "There's nowhere to go once you've been on Richard and Judy." However, keen to acquire new writing skills, she also wanted to adapt *Behind the Scenes* simply in order to learn how to write a screenplay.

She found writing a screenplay vastly different to fiction, not least because "knowing what's going to happen is very boring," and adapting *Behind the Scenes* posed several challenges. While *Abandonment* taught her much about how to write dialogue, Atkinson felt she still had a great deal to learn. As the novel contains relatively little speech, new dialogue had to be written, especially for scenes from the past. She also found it difficult making Ruby, defined largely by her voice in the novel, a three dimensional character. The impossibility of using a sustained first person narrative on television means that the world is no longer seen through Ruby's eyes and the sense of intimacy generated by her voice is lost as Ruby becomes one character among a cast of others. Atkinson decided to use voiceover to bring in Ruby's voice at key moments, which means if she remains a narrator at all, she is now a reliable narrator. Although Atkinson started out being precious about the novel and wanted to keep everything from the novel in the screenplay, she learned to be ruthless about making cuts and changes. Eventually, she abandoned the book altogether and views this approach to adaptation philosophically: "it was more an exercise in learning to write for TV than transferring *Behind the Scenes* into another medium without losing anything of the original." Atkinson's comments suggest that the BBC drama will constitute a quite different *Behind the Scenes*, rather than simply *Behind the Scenes* in another form. The novel and screenplay thus promise to be two quite different works of art.

5

Further Reading and Discussion Questions

QUESTIONS

The following questions are designed to prompt further reflection on themes and issues explored in previous chapters and expand the reader's consideration of the novel in new ways.

1. What is the significance of the novel's many references to "magical" objects and places, and repetition of the phrase "as if by magic"?

2. What is the significance of Bunty's dustbin dream?

3. In what ways is Bunty like a parrot?

4. What does the repetition of "just Ruby" suggest about Ruby's self-image?

5. How does Patricia's reading matter, which includes Sterne's *Tristram Shandy*, Smollett's *Humphry Clinker*, and Proust's *A Remembrance of Things Past*, reflect the novel's central concerns?

6. Georgia Jones-Davis remarked that *Behind the Scenes* " 'out-Copperfields' *David Copperfield*" (*Los Angeles Times*). In what ways is Atkinson's novel similar and different to *David Copperfield* — and *Great Expectations*?

7. What is the function of the multiple references to *Gone with the Wind*?

8. What is the significance of Ruby's museum dream?

9. How does the novel disrupt the linear process of reading as well as the linearity of historical time?

10. What does Atkinson's treatment of history have in common with Livy's *History of Rome*?

11. While nursing a doll, Ada's face assumes "an expression of maternal piety rarely seen outside the Nativity" (p. 29). What part does Christianity play in constructing myths of motherhood?

12. How are Patricia and Doreen affected by patriarchal myths of motherhood that idealize and demonize particular kinds of mother?

13. What does the novel's portrayal of the young Berenice who works at Modelia fashions and Bunty the grandmother who visits Australia suggest about the part that cultural conditions play in shaping identity and behavior?

14. In what ways do Ruby and Bunty eventually swap roles? What is the significance of this shift?

15. Why can Ruby only accept Bunty after her death?

16. In what ways does Alison represent historical change and development?

17. In what sense is Mrs. Roper "very English" (p. 233)?

18. Why is Auntie Eliza's friendship with "a couple from Jamaica" taboo (p. 79)?

19. What is the significance of references to the Roman Emperor Constantine, the Railway King, George Hudson, and Richard of York (p. 19)?

20. When Ruby asserts her Scottishness, she states, "I belong by blood to this foreign country," and emphasizes "the true Scottishness of the Lennoxes" (p. 381). How is this apparently essentialist conception of national identity undercut my Atkinson's representation of Scotland and Scottishness throughout the novel?

FURTHER READING

Postmodernism

Readers who wish to develop their understanding of postmodernism will find the following books useful: Robert Alter, *Partial Magic: The Novel as a Self-Conscious Genre* (1975); Patricia Waugh, *Metafiction: The Theory and Practice of Self-Conscious Fiction* (1984) and *Feminine Fictions: Revisiting the Postmodern* (1989); Brian McHale, *Postmodernist Fiction* (1987); Linda Hutcheon, *A Poetics of Postmodernism: History, Theory, Fiction* (1988) and *The Politics of Postmodernism* (1989); Alison Lee, *Realism and Power: Postmodern British Fiction* (1990); Madan Sarup, *An Introductory Guide to Post-Structuralism and Postmodernism* (1993); Mark Currie, *Postmodern Narrative Theory* (1998).

Realism, Fantasy and Fairy Tales

Readers interested in fairy tales might enjoy Angela Carter's *The Bloody Chamber* (1979) and Jeanette Winterson's *Sexing the Cherry* (1989), which revise traditional fairy tales in order to expose their patriarchal bias. Like *Behind the Scenes*, Muriel Spark's *The Girls of Slender Means* (1963) hovers between realism and fairy tale. Novels that draw on fantasy, seamlessly mixing the marvelous and the mundane, include Isabel Allende's magical family saga spanning four generations of South American women, *The House of the Spirits* (Spain, 1982), Fay Weldon's *The Life and Loves of a She-Devil* (1983), and Laura Esquivel's *Like Water for Chocolate* (1992). For a critical discussion of fantasy see Rosemary Jackson's *Fantasy: The Literature of Subversion* (1981), and Lucy Armitt's *Theorising the Fantastic* (1996).

Narratives of Female Development

The quest for identity is perhaps the most pervasive theme in contemporary women's writing. Sylvia Plath's *The Bell Jar* (1963) and Erica Jong's *Fanny: Being the True History of the Adventures of Fanny Hackabout-Jones* (1980) are two classic examples of the feminist "bildungsroman", the latter of which is written in the style of an eighteen century picaresque. Paule Marshall's *Brown Girl, Brownstones* (1959), Maya Angelou's *I Know Why the Caged Bird Sings* (1969), Toni Morrison's *The Bluest Eye* (1970) and Alice Walker's *The Color Purple* (1982) portray an African American experience of growing up female and explore the way that issues of race, class, and culture shape a young girl's sense of self. Jeanette Winterson's *Oranges Are Not the Only Fruit* (1985), a tragicomic fictional autobiography that features a heroine whose sexuality becomes a source of family conflict, places the narrative of female development in a British context, as does Meera Syal's *Anita and Me* (1996), which explores identity and self-definition from an Asian perspective. Although none of the following books discuss *Behind the Scenes* specifically, they provide a useful critical context in which to consider Atkinson's novel: Elizabeth Abel at el., *The Voy-*

age In: Fictions of Female Development (1983), Susan Fraiman, *Unbecoming Women: British Women Writers and the Novel of Development* (1993), and Ruth O. Saxton ed., *The Girl: Constructions of the Girl in Contemporary Fictions by Women* (1998).

Mother-Daughter Relations

A staple subject of writing by women, particularly since the rise of the Women's Movement in the 1960s. Many of the novels listed above explore the relationship between mothers and daughters but Margaret Atwood's *Lady Oracle* (1976) offers a particularly insightful account of the ambivalent character of mother-daughter relations. Amy Tan's *The Joy Luck Club* (1989) and Rebecca Wells' *Divine Secrets of the Ya-Ya Sisterhood* (1996) focus on daughters who gain insights into their own identities and come to understand and accept their mothers as they learn about the past. In addition to the texts by Rich, Nice, and Oakley cited below, the following provide stimulating insights into current debates on the subject: Marianne Hirsch, *The Mother/Daughter Plot: Narrative, Psychoanalysis, Feminism* (1989); Shelley Phillips, *Beyond the Myths: Mother-Daughter Relationships in Psychology, History, Literature and Everyday Life* (1991); Andrea O'Reilly and Sharon Abbey ed., *Mothers and Daughters: Connection, Empowerment, Transformation* (2000); Hilary S. Crew, *Is it Really Mommie Dearest: Daughter-Mother Narratives in Young Adult Fiction* (2000); Roberta Rubenstein, *Home Matters: Longing and Belonging, Nostalgia and Mourning in Women's Fiction* (2001).

Memory

Like *Behind the Scenes*, Toni Morrison's *Beloved* (1987) explores a legacy of loss and the pain of coming to terms with traumatic memories of the past, but does so in a quite different context, that of slavery. Repressed memory occurs in fiction with increasing frequency throughout the 1990s. Jane Smiley's *A Thousand Acres* (1991) features recovered memories of sexual abuse, Michèle Roberts's *Daughters of the House* (1992) revolves around childhood memories of the postwar period and secrets relating to the Holocaust, Helen Dunmore's *Talking to the Dead* (1996) concerns sisters, family secrets, and repressed memories of a sibling's death, and Margaret Forster's *The Memory Box* (1999) is a novel that employs objects to explore repressed memories and mother-daughter-relations. In addition to Nicola King's book cited below, readers will find valuable discussions of memory in Peter Middleton and Tim Woods' *Literatures of Memory: History, Time and Space in Postwar Writing* (2000) and Nancy J. Peterson's *Against Amnesia: Contemporary Women Writers and the Crises of Historical Memory* (2001).

History

Other novels that take a revisionary look at war include Sebastian Faulks' *Birdsong* (1993) and Pat Barker's *Regeneration Trilogy* (1992–1995). As historical novels based on true stories, Jane Rogers *Mr. Wroe's Virgins* (1991) and Margaret Atwood's *Alias Grace* (1996) rescue women lost in time. Salman Rushdie's *Midnight's Children* (1981), Angela Carter's *Nights at the Circus* (1984), Julian Barnes' *A History of the World in 10½ Chapters* (1989), and several novels by Jeanette Winterson including *The Passion* (1987) and *Sexing the Cherry* (1989) erode the boundary between fact and fiction, and offer examples of what Linda Hutcheon calls "historiographic metafiction." For useful background reading see Robert Holton's *Jarring Witnesses: Modern Fiction and the Representation of History* (1994) and Steven Connor's *The English Novel in History, 1950–1995* (1996).

Englishness

The 1990s gave rise to a number of novels that challenge the dominant ideology of Englishness. *Behind the Scenes* joins Kazuo Ishiguro's *The Remains of the Day* (1989), Graham Swift's *Last Orders* (1996), and Julian Barnes' *England, England* (1998) in deconstructing myths of Englishness. In addition to the texts listed in the Works Cited, David Gervais' *Literary Englands: Versions of Englishness in Modern Writing* (1993), Menno Spiering's *Englishness: Foreigners and Images of National Identity in Postwar Literature* (1992), Ian A. Bell's *Peripheral Visions: Images of Nationhood in Contemporary British Fiction* (1995), and essays in Tracey Hill and William Hughes' *Contemporary Writing and National Identity* (1995) offer insightful discussions of representations of England and the construction of Englishness. Readers who wish to pursue debates about national identity from a feminist perspective will benefit from Nira Yuval-Davis' *Gender and Nation* (1997).

BIBLIOGRAPHY

Works by Kate Atkinson

Novels

Behind the Scenes at the Museum. London: Doubleday, 1995; New York: St Martin's Press, 1996.

Human Croquet. London: Doubleday, 1997. New York: Picador USA, 1998.

Emotionally Weird. London: Doubleday, 2000. New York: Picador USA, 2000.

Plays and Screenplays

Abandonment. Dir. John Tiffany. Traverse Theatre, Edinburgh, 11 July 2000. London: Nick Hearn, 2000.

Karmic Mothers. Dir. John Tiffany. BBC 2, 1996.

Nice. Dir. John Tiffany. Traverse Theatre, Edinburgh, 31 May–9 June 1996.

Short Stories

"In China." *Woman's Own*, 1988.

"Leaves of Light." *The Scotsman*, 1996.

"Inner Balance." *The Catch: Prize Winning Stories by Women*. Carole Buchan ed. London: Serpent's Tale, 1997.

"This Dog's Life." *Daily Mail*, January 7, 1997.

"Karmic Mothers = Fact or Fiction?" *Snap Shots: 10 Years of the Ian St James Awards*. Tunbridge Wells: Angela Royal Publishing, 1999.

"A Partner for Life." *Daily Express*, March 12, 2000.

"The Body's Vest." *Daily Telegraph*, March 17, 2001.

"Small Mercies." *Good Housekeeping*, December 2001.

Miscellaneous

Kate Atkinson and Merric Davidson ed. *Pleasure Vessels: Winning Entries from the Ian St. James Award for New Fiction*. London: Angela Royal Publishing, 1997.

Interviews and Reviews:

Alberge, Dalya. "First Novel Beats Rushdie." *The Times*, January 24, 1996.
———. "Give Me the Boring Life, Says Literary World's Newest Star." *The Times*, January 25, 1996.

Barton, Geoff. "Sex, Satire and Society." *Times Educational Supplement*, July 19, 1996.

Benedict, David. "The Life Of Bryony." *The Independent*, January 19, 2001.

Bergonzi, Bernard. "Critics' Choices for Christmas." *Commonweal*, December 6, 1996.

Billington, Michael. "Review: Abandonment." *The Guardian*, August 7, 2000.

Bruce, Keith. "Family Saga First Novel Wins Whitbread Award." *The Herald*, Glasgow, January 3, 1996.

Bunce, Kim. "Emotionally Weird? Moi?." *The Guardian*, March 12, 2000.

Clark, Alex. "The Fragility of Goodness." *The Guardian*, March 10, 2001.

———. "Wag tales." *The Guardian*, March 11, 2000.

Cleave, Maureen. "Maker of Happy Endings." *Daily Telegraph*, March 8, 1997.

Conaghan, Dan. "Family Saga Beats the Odds To Win Whitbread." *Daily Telegraph*, January 24, 1996.

Corrigan, Sue. "It's Your funeral." *Night and Day*, a supplement to *The Mail on Sunday*, March 4, 2001.

Coveney, Michael. "Museum Piece Worth Inspecting." *Daily Mail* (available on the web at *www.femail.co.uk*).

Crampton, Robert. "Weird and Emotional." *The Times Magazine*, March 4, 2000.

Critchley, Julian. "Why Roy Jenkins Was Robbed." *Daily Telegraph*, January 25, 1996.

Diary. "Dream On, Ye Spires." *The Independent*, January 29,1996.

Dickson, Jane. "Sanity Through the Looking Glass." *The Times*, February 24, 2001.

D.S. "N.B." *Times Literary Supplement*, February 2, 1996.

Ellison, Mike. "Rushdie Makes It a Losing Double." *The Guardian*, January 24, 1996.

Goring, Rosemary. "Black Not Blue." *Scotland on Sunday*, January 7, 1996.

Jones-Davis, Georgia. "From the Mouth of a Babe, the Details of Ordinary Lives." *Los Angeles Times*, December 27, 1995.

Kelly, Jane. "What is the point of men—who needs them?" *Daily Mail*, January 25, 1996.

Louden, Mary. "An Exhibition of Herself." *The Times*, December 30, 1995.
———. "Family of the Century." *The Times*, March 18, 1995.

MacDonald, Marianne. "First-timer Wins Book of the Year." *The Independent*, January 24, 1996.

McDowell, Lesley. "Behind the Scenes At a Novelist's First Performance." *The Independent*, July 30, 2000.

McKay, Alastair. "I Want To Be Alone." *The Scotsman Weekend*, March 8, 1997.

Macintyre, Ben. "Yorkshire Terrors." *The New York Times Book Review*, March 31, 1996.

Mann, Jesssica. "Wit Loses Out To Whimsy." *Daily Telegraph*, March 22, 1997.

Mantel, Hilary. "Shop!" *London Review of Books*, April 4, 1996.

Neil, Andrew. "All Chattering—But No Class." *Daily Mail*, January 25, 1996.

Porlock, Harvey. "Critical List." *The Sunday Times*, February 4, 1996.

Rigby, Sarah. "Behind the Scenes at the Museum." *Times Literary Supplement*, April 21, 1995.

Rubin, Merle. "New Voices Spin Tales of Fiction, Mostly Fiction." *Christian Science Monitor*, January 10, 1996.

Staples, Sally. "Families To Love and Hate." *Sunday Express*, March 12, 1995.

Tabor, Mary B.W. "Rushdie Takes 2nd Prize." *The New York Times*, January 24, 1996.

Traugott, Maggie. "Review." *Independent on Sunday*, April 9, 1995.

Tressider, Megan. "Big Sister of the Anti-family." *The Guardian*, January 27, 1996.

Walker, Lynn. "Behind the Scenes with Kate Atkinson." *The Independent*, August 7, 2000.

Walter, Natasha. "Writer Who Hears Her Own Music." *Mail and Guardian*, South Africa, June 4, 1997.

Woodward, Tim. "Nostalgic Thread of Scribblings in the Dark." *Yorkshire Post*, March 9, 1995.

Websites

Kate Atkinson is currently constructing her own official website. The "Wonderful" Unofficial Kate Atkinson Website, which contains general information, news, reviews and a discussion board, can be found at *www.geocities.com/kateatkinson14*.

Kate Atkinson's Top Ten is posted on *The Guardian*'s website: *www.books.guradian.co.uk/top10s*.

General information and an interview by James Naughtie for BBC Radio 4's *Book Club* can be found at *www.bbc.co.uk/education/bookcase/bookclub/atkinson*.

For interviews, see *www.amazon.com/exec/obidos/show-interview/a-k/tkins* and *www.salon.com/30dec1995/sneakpeaks*.

Several sites offer a summary of the novel and further questions for discussion:

www.booksattransworld.co.uk

www.bloomsburymagazine.com

www.redinggroupguides.com/guides/behind the_scenes_at_the_museum.html

www.whatamigoingtoread.com/books/book_review215.htm

Works Cited

Anderson, Benedict. *Imagined Communities: Reflections on the Origin and Spread of Nationalism*. 1983. London: Verso, 1991.

Atwood, Margaret. *Second Words: Selected Critical Prose*. Toronto: Anansi, 1982.

Bhabha, Homi. *The Location of Culture*. London: Routledge, 1994.

Boccaccio, Giovanni. *Famous Women*. Trans. Virginia Brown. Cambridge, Mass.: Harvard University Press, 2001.

Booth, Wayne. *The Rhetoric of Fiction*. Chicago: University of Chicago Press, 1961.

Chase, Richard. *The American Novel and its Tradition*. New York: Anchor Books, 1957.

Easthope, Antony. *Englishness and National Culture*. London: Routledge, 1999.

Freud, Sigmund. *The Standard Edition of the Complete Psychological Works of Sigmund Freud*. Trans. and ed. James Strachey. 24 vols. London: The Hogarth Press, 1953–74.

King, Nicola. *Memory, Narrative, Identity: Remembering the Self*. Edinburgh: Edinburgh University Press, 2000.

Light, Alison. *Forever England: Femininity, Literature and Conservatism Between the Wars*. London: Routledge, 1991.

Lodge, David. *The Art of Fiction*. London: Penguin, 1992.

Marshall, Paule. "The Making of a Writer: From the Poets in the Kitchen" in *Reena and Other Stories*. New York: Feminist Press, 1983.

McLeod, John. *Beginning Postcolonialism*. Manchester: Manchester University Press, 2000.

Middleton, Tim and Judy Giles, eds. *Writing Englishness 1900–1950*. London: Routledge, 1995.

Morris, Nigel. "Hague Disowns Tory MP Who Blames Refugees For Soaring Crime." *The Independent*, March 28, 2001.

Nice, Vivien E. *Mothers and Daughters: The Distortion of a Relationship*. Basingstoke: Macmillan, 1992.

Oakley, Ann. *Woman's Work: The Housewife Past and Present*. New York: Pantheon, 1974. Published in Britain as *Housewife*. London: Allen Lane, 1974.

Paxman, Jeremy. *The English: A Portrait of a People*. London: Michael Joseph, 1998.

Rich, Adrienne. *Of Woman Born: Motherhood as Experience and Institution*. London: Virago, 1977.

Rushdie, Salman. *Imaginary Homelands: Essays and Criticism 1981–1991*. London: Granta, 1991.

———. *The Wizard of Oz*. London: British Film Institute, 1992.

Thatcher, Margaret. "Aids, Education and the Year 2000." *Woman's Own*, October 3, 1987.

Wall, Kathleen. "The Remains of the Day and its Challenges to Theories of Unreliable Narration" in *The Journal of Narrative Technique* 24:1, Winter 1994: 18–42.

Warner, Marina. *From the Beast to the Blonde: On Fairy Tales and Their Tellers*. London: Chatto and Windus, 1994.

White, Hayden. *Tropics of Discourse: Essays in Cultural Criticism*. Baltimore: Johns Hopkins University Press, 1978.

Wittig, Monique. *The Straight Mind and Other Essays*. Hemel Hempstead: Harvester Wheatsheaf, 1992.

Woolf, Virginia. *A Room of One's Own and Three Guineas*. Michèle Barrett ed. London: Penguin, 1993.

Zipes, Jack. *Breaking the Magic Spell: Radical Theories of Folk and Fairy Tales*. Austin: Texas, 1979.

———. *When Dreams Come True: Classical Fairy Tales and Their Tradition*. London: Routledge, 1999.